Copyright © 2025 ND Publishing
All rights reserved.
ISBN: 9798287467647

No part of this publication may be reproduced, distributed, or transmitted in any form or by any means—electronic, mechanical, photocopying, recording, or otherwise—without the prior written permission of the publisher, except in the case of brief quotations embodied in critical reviews and certain other noncommercial uses permitted by copyright law.

This book is a work of nonfiction based on historical research and publicly available information. While every effort has been made to ensure accuracy, the author and publisher make no representations or warranties regarding the completeness, reliability, or accuracy of the content. The information is provided "as is" and is subject to revision in light of new discoveries or interpretations.

This book is intended for educational and informational purposes only. It does not provide military, political, or strategic advice. The views expressed are those of the author and do not necessarily reflect those of any organization, institution, or government.

All trademarks, service marks, and trade names mentioned in this book are the property of their respective owners. Any resemblance to actual people, living or dead, is purely coincidental unless otherwise noted as historical figures.

	1
Chapter 1: Why Ancient Chinese Warfare Still Matters	9
1.1 Foundations of Chinese Military Thought	9
Origins and Key Concepts	9
Strategic Over Tactical Thinking	9
Influence Beyond China	10
Warfare as Philosophy	10
Warfare and Empire-Building	11
1.2 Defining the Timeline	11
Key Dynastic Periods	11
Patterns in Military Evolution	13
Influence of Foreign Threats	13
1.3 What You'll Learn in This Book	14
Tactical Systems and Battlefield Logic	14
Legendary Generals and Campaigns	15
Practical Takeaways for Modern Readers	16
Chapter 2: The Warrior Kings of Early China	18
2.1 The Shang and Zhou Periods	18
Ritual Warfare and Bronze Power	18
The Rise of Feudal Warlords	18
Fortifications and Defensive Rituals	19
2.2 Technology in the Bronze Age	20
Bronze Weaponry and Armor	20
Chariots and Mobility	20
Early Command Structures	21
2.3 Transition to the Warring States	22
Political Fragmentation	22
Military Competition	23
Reforms and Innovation	23
Chapter 3: The Warring States and the Age of Reform	25
3.1 The Seven Powers	25
The Seven Warring States	25

Arms Escalation	26
Evolution of Generalship	26
3.2 Qin's Military Advantage	**27**
Shang Yang's Reforms	28
Mass Conscription	28
Technological Superiority	29
3.3 The Final Conquests	**30**
Zhao and the Elite Cavalry	30
Siege of Handan and Deception	30
Unification Under Qin	31
Chapter 4: The Qin Dynasty and Total War	**33**
4.1 Rise of a Centralized Army	**33**
Abolishment of Noble-Led Forces	33
Standardization	33
Infrastructure for War	34
4.2 The Campaigns of Conquest	**35**
Against Chu and Qi	35
Internal Suppression	36
Engineering as Warfare	37
4.3 Fall of the Qin	**38**
Overextension	38
Peasant Rebellions	38
The Death of a Dynasty	39
Lessons in Leadership Failure	39
Chapter 5: Han Dynasty—Tactics of a Rising Empire	**41**
5.1 Rebuilding the Army	**41**
From Rebels to Rulers	41
Creation of a Professional Force	41
Balancing Civil and Military Power	42
5.2 Expansion and Diplomacy	**43**
Han–Xiongnu Wars	43
Silk Road Defense	44
Han in the South	44
5.3 Military Innovations	**45**
Repeating Crossbows	45
Horse-Mounted Archery	46

Logistics and Supply Chains	46
Chapter 6: Three Kingdoms—Warlords and Master Strategists	**48**
6.1 The Collapse of Han	**48**
Fragmentation of Power	48
Rise of Cao Cao	49
Sun Quan and Liu Bei	49
6.2 Iconic Battles	**50**
The Battle of Guandu (200 CE)	50
The Battle of Red Cliffs (208–209 CE)	51
Hanzhong Campaign (217–219 CE)	51
6.3 Zhuge Liang's Legacy	**53**
Strategy Through Adaptation	53
Inventions and Tools	53
Death and Decline	54
Chapter 7: Jin and the Age of Decline	**56**
7.1 Post-Three Kingdoms Disorder	**56**
Internal Weakening	56
Barbarian Incursions	56
Collapse of Central Command	57
7.2 Southern Survival	**58**
Flight to the South	58
Defensive Adaptations	59
Attempts at Reunification	59
7.3 Lessons from Decline	**60**
Overreliance on Elites	60
Resistance to Reform	61
Vulnerability to Outsiders	61
Chapter 8: Sui and Tang—The Return of Imperial Might	**63**
8.1 Sui Unification Campaigns	**63**
Grand Canal and Troop Movement	63
Crushing Southern Resistance	63
Korean Invasion Failure	64
8.2 Tang Military System	**65**
Fubing Militia System	65
Command Hierarchy	66
Emphasis on Mobility	66

8.3 Frontier Expansion	67
Central Asia Campaigns	68
Tibet and the Western Campaigns	68
Internal Rebellions	69
Chapter 9: Song Dynasty—Innovation Under Pressure	**70**
9.1 Military Challenges	**70**
Constant Northern Threats	70
Civilian Control of the Military	70
Internal Dissent and Structural Paralysis	71
9.2 Technological Breakthroughs	**72**
Gunpowder Weapons	72
Naval Dominance	73
Siege Engineering	73
9.3 Notable Defenses	**74**
Battle of Kaifeng	75
Border Skirmishes and Tactical Defense	75
Lessons from Defeat	76
Chapter 10: Yuan Dynasty—The Mongol War Machine	**78**
10.1 Khan's Invasion	**78**
Psychological Warfare	78
Speed and Maneuver	78
Local Adaptation	79
10.2 Kublai Khan's Empire	**80**
Sinicization of the Military	80
Naval Ambitions and Failed Invasions	81
Control Through Fear and Infrastructure	82
10.3 Mongol Military Legacy	**82**
Blended Tactics and Hybrid Army Culture	83
Strategic Weaknesses and Military Overreach	83
The End of Mongol Supremacy	84
Chapter 11: Ming Dynasty — Rebuilding from the Ashes	**86**
11.1 Restoring the Military System	**86**
Zhu Yuanzhang's Reforms	86
Revival of Native Pride	86
Problems with Central Control	87
11.2 Defensive Fortifications	**88**

Great Wall Reconstruction	88
Coastal Defense Systems	89
City Planning for War	90
11.3 Major Campaigns	**90**
Ming–Mongol Conflicts	91
The Imjin War (Korea)	91
Fall of the Dynasty	92
Chapter 12: Qing Dynasty — The Last Imperial Army	**94**
12.1 Manchu Military Origins	**94**
Banner System Organization	94
Conquest of China	95
Assimilation and Discipline	95
12.2 Stability through Control	**96**
Suppressing Internal Rebellions	96
Dual Military System: Banners and Green Standards	97
Border Expansion and Ethnic Control	98
12.3 Resistance to Change	**99**
Avoiding Western Modernization	99
Failures in Modernization	100
Military Collapse	100
Chapter 13: Weapons, Tools, and Technologies	**102**
13.1 Infantry and Cavalry Weapons	**102**
Swords and Halberds	102
Bows and Crossbows	103
Armor and Shields	103
13.2 Siege and Fortification Tech	**104**
Siege Engines	104
Wall Design and Layered Defenses	105
Defensive Countermeasures	106
13.3 Gunpowder and Naval Warfare	**107**
Fire Lances, Bombs, and Early Cannons	107
Cannons, Rockets, and Land-Based Artillery	108
Naval Advancements and Ship-Based Warfare	108
Chapter 14: The Philosophy of War in China	**110**
14.1 The Art of War and Its Legacy	**110**
Key Principles of Strategy	110

Historical Applications	110
Global Influence	111
14.2 Legalism and Confucian Tensions	**112**
Legalist Control and Command	112
Confucian Restraint and Moral Limits	113
Daoist Flexibility and Harmony	114
14.3 Strategic Thinking Across Eras	**114**
The General as Philosopher	115
Balance of Offense and Defense	115
The Role of Fate and Cosmic Signs	116
Chapter 15: Lessons for the Modern World	**118**
15.1 Timeless Military Principles	**118**
Adapt or Die	118
The Price of Stagnation	118
Learning from Failure	119
Intelligence Wins Battles	119
Psychological Edge and Non-Violent Victories	120
15.2 Cultural Memory of Warfare	**121**
National Pride and Trauma	121
Literature and Storytelling	121
Education and Modern Use	122
15.3 The Enduring Legacy	**123**
Influence on East Asian Warfare	123
Modern Parallels	124
China's Military Future	124

Chapter 1: Why Ancient Chinese Warfare Still Matters

1.1 Foundations of Chinese Military Thought

Sun Tzu and *The Art of War*

Long before tanks and satellites, long before Napoleon marched across Europe or Caesar crossed the Rubicon, Chinese thinkers were defining the rules of warfare—not just as a way to win battles, but as a tool to manage power, maintain order, and shape entire civilizations. At the heart of this strategic tradition stands one name: **Sun Tzu**.

Origins and Key Concepts

The Art of War, written around the 5th century BCE during the Warring States period, is not just a military manual. It's a blueprint for navigating chaos. Sun Tzu, likely a general or strategist in the state of Wu, condensed centuries of tactical knowledge into thirteen compact chapters. Each one explores a vital element of warfare—planning, deception, terrain, leadership, and more—but always with a focus on precision, control, and minimal destruction.

Sun Tzu didn't celebrate war. He studied it. He believed the highest form of skill wasn't to win 100 battles, but to win without fighting at all. He emphasized that war should be a last resort and that it must serve a purpose beyond conquest. Victory, for Sun Tzu, was about balance and long-term stability—not short-term bloodshed.

Strategic Over Tactical Thinking

Where many commanders focus on the battlefield—positioning troops, outflanking enemies, and counting casualties—Sun Tzu encourages readers to think upstream. His philosophy prioritizes *strategy over tactics*. In modern terms, it's like focusing more on the chessboard than the next move.

Know the terrain, know your enemy, and know yourself, he advises. Victory comes not from overwhelming force but from superior insight. Manipulating the opponent's perception, avoiding unnecessary conflict, and controlling the conditions of battle are all preferable to head-on assaults.

This way of thinking stood in sharp contrast to the brute-force traditions seen elsewhere in the ancient world. In Chinese military philosophy, intelligence, deception, and adaptability were not signs of cowardice, but of mastery.

Influence Beyond China

The reach of Sun Tzu's ideas didn't stop at China's borders. Over centuries, The Art of War spread throughout East Asia—becoming essential reading in Japan, Korea, and Vietnam. Samurai generals quoted it. Korean resistance fighters applied it. Even modern military academies around the world include it in leadership training.

Beyond the battlefield, its lessons have seeped into politics, sports, and business. CEOs, diplomats, and even NFL coaches have studied its lines: *"Appear weak when you are strong, and strong when you are weak."* In a world driven by competition and risk, Sun Tzu's principles offer a timeless edge.

Warfare as Philosophy

Chinese views of war have always intertwined with philosophy. While Sun Tzu represented a pragmatic approach, others debated the morality of warfare. **Confucianism**, for example, favored social harmony, hierarchy, and moral governance. War, in this context, was seen as a necessary evil—justified only when peace was threatened.

In contrast, **Legalist** thinkers like Shang Yang and Han Fei emphasized strict laws, centralized power, and militarized discipline. To them, war was a legitimate tool for enforcing order and expanding the state. Victory was proof of divine favor and strength.

Out of this tension arose the Chinese concept of a "just war"—not in the Western sense of righteousness, but one where conflict was used to restore balance, punish disorder, or enforce legitimacy.

Warfare and Empire-Building

Military power wasn't just about battles. It was a pillar of statecraft. Dynasties rose and fell based on their ability to organize, supply, and discipline their armies. From unifying warring kingdoms under the Qin to protecting the trade routes of the Han, warfare shaped China's borders and internal structure.

Wars were often used not just to destroy enemies, but to unify tribes, claim mandates, and cement political order. Where Western empires expanded through colonization, Chinese warfare was often about drawing fragmented powers into a centralized, ordered whole.

Understanding this mindset is the first step to understanding Chinese military history. It's not just a series of battles. It's a philosophical tradition—one where strategy is an art, victory is balance, and power is only respected when controlled.

1.2 Defining the Timeline

Understanding ancient Chinese warfare means more than memorizing a list of battles or names. To truly grasp the logic behind the decisions, strategies, and technologies, you need a sense of *when and why* these changes occurred. China's military history spans over 3,000 years, and it's shaped by three major phases: **pre-imperial**, **imperial rise**, and the **late empire**. Each period reflects a shift not only in weapons and tactics, but also in the very meaning of power and control.

Key Dynastic Periods

Pre-Imperial (Shang and Zhou):
China's earliest dynasties, particularly the Shang (c. 1600–1046 BCE) and the Zhou (c. 1046–256 BCE), laid the groundwork for Chinese military culture. Warfare during this era was often ceremonial and aristocratic. Battles were fought by elite chariot units supported by spearmen and archers. Combat was localized, tied to feudal disputes between noble houses, and closely linked with religious rituals and ancestral honor.

During the later Zhou period, the Warring States era erupted—a chaotic time when regional powers began professionalizing their militaries, introducing iron weapons, and embracing merit-based promotions. It was during this era that thinkers like Sun Tzu emerged, trying to make sense of this constant violence with lasting philosophical frameworks.

Imperial Rise (Qin to Tang):

The unification of China under the Qin Dynasty (221–206 BCE) marked a dramatic military transformation. The Qin introduced centralized military command, abolished noble armies, and implemented mass conscription. Warfare became more organized, larger in scale, and increasingly strategic. The Han (206 BCE – 220 CE) further refined this model, creating long-range campaigns, developing cavalry to confront steppe raiders, and building infrastructure like roads and walls to move armies quickly.

The Tang Dynasty (618–907 CE) marked the high point of Chinese imperial military power. With vast cavalry forces and frontier garrisons, the Tang projected power deep into Central Asia, dominating trade routes and influencing neighboring kingdoms. Their armies became a model of multicultural cooperation, drawing recruits from across the empire and beyond.

Late Empire (Song to Qing):

In the Song Dynasty (960–1279 CE), China saw extraordinary technological innovation, but military setbacks. Surrounded by powerful nomadic rivals, the Song leaned heavily on gunpowder, naval innovation, and advanced city defenses. However, political mistrust of generals weakened their war-readiness.

The Mongol-led Yuan Dynasty (1271–1368) brought the brutal steppe model of warfare—fast cavalry, mobile archers, and psychological warfare—into the heart of China. The Ming (1368–1644) and Qing (1644–1912) dynasties tried to restore Chinese dominance, but military decline set in. By the Qing era, China's army had become bloated and resistant to reform, leaving it vulnerable to Western powers by the 19th century.

Patterns in Military Evolution

Across these periods, a few consistent patterns emerge:

- **From Decentralized to Centralized Command:**
  Early Chinese warfare was dominated by feudal lords and clan-based armies. But over time, as emperors consolidated power, the military became an arm of the state. By the Qin, nobles were stripped of command and replaced by appointed generals loyal to the center. This centralization allowed for larger, more coordinated campaigns—but also made the empire vulnerable when that central leadership faltered.

- **Rise of Cavalry and Gunpowder:**
  China's early reliance on infantry and chariots gave way to a more mobile, horse-centered warfare in response to northern nomadic threats. By the Song era, gunpowder became a decisive factor, used in grenades, fire lances, and eventually cannons. While revolutionary, these advances often outpaced battlefield doctrine, leading to missed opportunities.

- **Shift from Feudal Lords to Standing Armies:**
  As the empire matured, the reliance on nobles and peasant militias faded. The state began funding permanent garrisons, formal training, and professional commanders. This shift allowed dynasties like the Tang and Ming to maintain vast borders—but it also meant high costs and political risks, especially when powerful generals gained popularity.

Influence of Foreign Threats

China's military evolution didn't happen in a vacuum. Foreign threats played a key role in shaping strategies and reforms:

- **Nomadic Pressure:**
  The Xiongnu, Mongols, and later the Manchu were not just raiders—they were organized, effective enemies who forced China to adapt or fall. In response, the Chinese developed cavalry tactics, expanded the Great Wall, and negotiated with

steppe powers using tribute, trade, or war.

- **Maritime Concerns:**
  In later dynasties, especially during the Song and Ming, piracy and naval threats from Japan and Southeast Asia forced the creation of coastal defenses and riverine fleets. Maritime power became essential, even if underappreciated by land-focused officials.

- **Encounters with the West:**
  By the 19th century, encounters with European powers revealed how far China's military had fallen behind. Rifled guns, steam-powered ships, and industrial logistics shattered the illusion of Chinese invincibility and marked the beginning of a painful but necessary reevaluation.

1.3 What You'll Learn in This Book

Warfare is more than just battle—it's the sharpest tool in a state's arsenal. In ancient China, it wasn't simply about crushing enemies. War built empires, tested rulers, and exposed the true strengths and weaknesses of a nation. By the time you finish this book, you'll not only know what happened, but *how* it happened, *why* it mattered, and *what* it still teaches us today.

This guide is structured to help you connect the dots between tactics and philosophy, generals and empires, victories and collapses. Each chapter will introduce systems, stories, and strategies that shaped China's military evolution—and still echo in modern power struggles.

Tactical Systems and Battlefield Logic

Chinese warfare developed its own distinct set of methods and logic, shaped by terrain, politics, and philosophy. You'll explore the evolution of **infantry, cavalry, siegecraft**, and **naval warfare**—each with its own unique doctrines and innovations.

- **Infantry:** From bronze-armed foot soldiers in the Shang dynasty to the conscripted armies of the Han and Ming, infantry remained the backbone of many campaigns. We'll look at formations, weapons, and training systems.

- **Cavalry:** The response to nomadic threats shaped some of China's most powerful cavalry traditions. You'll see how mounted archery and fast flanking tactics changed everything from recruitment to battlefield speed.

- **Siege and Naval Warfare:** Whether storming walled cities with towers and battering rams, or turning rivers into firetraps as at Red Cliffs, Chinese armies excelled in adapting to complex environments. You'll learn how engineers, ships, and climate often decided outcomes more than swords did.

We'll also unpack the environmental and strategic factors: **terrain**, **weather**, and especially **deception**. Ancient commanders learned to weaponize fog, floods, and false information just as effectively as spears and arrows.

Legendary Generals and Campaigns

Behind every great battle is a great mind—or a colossal mistake. Throughout this book, you'll meet legendary figures who didn't just win wars—they *redefined* them.

- **The Decision-Makers:** From Sun Tzu's philosophy of subtle control to Cao Cao's cold pragmatism, from Zhuge Liang's brilliant logistics to Yue Fei's loyalty, China produced an extraordinary range of military minds. Each general faced different enemies, environments, and political challenges.

- **Turning Points:** You'll explore decisive moments in history—like the unification under Qin, the fire tactics of Red Cliffs, the Mongol conquest of the Song, and the Ming resistance against Japanese invasions. These weren't just military victories, they were national redefinitions.

- **Stories That Shaped a Nation:** Some campaigns became legend, some became warnings. All of them offer insight into what Chinese leadership valued—discipline, harmony, patience, or raw force.

These generals and campaigns won't just be names and dates. You'll learn *why* they chose certain strategies, *how* they adapted to challenges, and *what* their choices reveal about China's larger worldview.

Practical Takeaways for Modern Readers

This isn't just about history. Each chapter is designed to leave you with clear, memorable insights that you can apply far beyond the battlefield.

- **Timeless Strategy:** Many of the principles in Chinese warfare are still studied in business schools, military academies, and political campaigns. The value of timing, misdirection, and preparation never goes out of style.

- **Leadership Lessons:** From handling difficult terrain to commanding untrustworthy allies, ancient Chinese generals dealt with every form of pressure. Their victories—and especially their failures—offer lessons in responsibility, loyalty, and calculated risk.

- **Cultural Resilience:** One of the deepest takeaways is how China survived so many wars and still held together. The ability to recover, reorganize, and adapt is a core theme of this book. Understanding that resilience gives you a clearer view of how China thinks today—strategically, socially, and politically.

By the end, you won't just have a timeline of battles in your head. You'll walk away with a strategist's mindset, a historian's depth, and a clearer understanding of one of the world's oldest military traditions.

Chapter 2: The Warrior Kings of Early China

2.1 The Shang and Zhou Periods

Ritual Warfare and the Rise of Feudal Power

Before the sweeping armies and grand campaigns of imperial China, warfare was smaller, symbolic, and deeply intertwined with religion and class. In the Shang and early Zhou periods (roughly 1600–771 BCE), war was less about conquest and more about *display*—a ritual of power between elite clans. Understanding this early phase helps explain how military culture evolved from noble duels to total war.

Ritual Warfare and Bronze Power

In the Shang dynasty, warfare was dominated by bronze—both as a tool of death and a symbol of status. Bronze was expensive, difficult to produce, and controlled by the ruling elite. Swords, axes, and spearheads were ornately cast, sometimes inscribed with family names or divine blessings. These weapons weren't just functional—they were sacred objects tied to ancestor worship and heavenly approval.

The battlefield was equally ceremonial. Shang kings led small, organized forces into combat, often in the form of chariot warfare. These wooden, two-wheeled vehicles were drawn by horses and manned by elite warriors—usually a driver, a spearman, and an archer. The clash of chariots wasn't chaotic like later infantry battles. It was structured and stylized, resembling a deadly parade that reinforced the social hierarchy.

Combat wasn't just about winning. It was about **displaying divine favor**. Victory confirmed the Shang king's connection to the heavens. Losers might be captured, sacrificed, or absorbed into the victors' ancestral rites. War was public, performative, and heavily ritualized.

The Rise of Feudal Warlords

After the fall of the Shang, the Zhou dynasty introduced a new political structure: feudalism. The Zhou kings granted land to loyal nobles, who in turn pledged military service. This system decentralized power, and over time, those nobles began acting like kings themselves.

Each noble clan controlled its own territory, taxed its own people, and raised its own army. These **private armies** were composed of elite charioteers, foot soldiers, and sometimes mercenaries. Warfare between these lords became increasingly common—not just to settle disputes, but to gain territory and prestige.

As central Zhou authority weakened, especially during the Spring and Autumn period (770–476 BCE), alliances shifted constantly. Vassals betrayed overlords, coalitions formed and broke apart, and warfare became a constant feature of life. Unlike the earlier Shang model, war was no longer a ritual—it was political.

This transition laid the groundwork for the **Warring States period**, where seven major powers would battle for dominance in increasingly brutal and innovative ways.

Fortifications and Defensive Rituals

Early Chinese city-states were walled, not only to defend against invaders but to symbolize civilization itself. A city without walls was vulnerable, both physically and spiritually. These walls, usually built from rammed earth, were thick and steep, with wooden gates and towers for surveillance.

While siege warfare was still in its infancy, basic techniques like moat-digging, battering rams, and fires were used. However, many battles were still resolved in open field engagements between noble forces. The idea of prolonged sieges came later, as cities grew in size and strategic importance.

Defense also included **ritual protection**. Omens were read, sacrifices made, and ancestral spirits invoked before a battle. Commanders sought divine signs—eclipses, dreams, animal behavior—to determine when to fight or retreat. Military decisions were deeply tied to cosmic interpretation.

These early beliefs weren't superstitions in the modern sense—they were a core part of how rulers justified their actions. Victory wasn't just skill. It was a sign of Heaven's favor

2.2 Technology in the Bronze Age

Weapons, Chariots, and the Early Mechanics of War

The foundation of early Chinese military power was not size or speed—it was **bronze**. In the Shang and early Zhou periods, bronze wasn't just a metal, it was a statement. Those who controlled bronze controlled warfare. As a result, military technology became both a physical and political tool, giving shape to the first generations of Chinese armies.

Bronze Weaponry and Armor

Crafting bronze required precision. The alloy, made from copper and tin, had to be smelted at high temperatures and cast in molds. This made weapon production time-consuming and expensive, which is why it remained in the hands of the ruling elite. Blacksmiths weren't simply laborers—they were essential to power.

The **weapons** themselves were impressive for the time. Swords (*jian*), daggers, spears, and battle-axes were the most common tools of war. Many carried intricate inscriptions or stylized motifs of tigers, dragons, or taotie masks, suggesting that these weapons were also ritual objects meant to please the ancestors or the gods.

But bronze had its **limits**. It dulled quickly, snapped under too much force, and was ineffective against harder materials like iron, which would emerge centuries later. Bronze armor, typically in the form of helmets and breastplates, offered some protection, but was too heavy and costly for wide distribution. This meant most armor was reserved for nobles and charioteers—common soldiers often fought with little more than cloth and courage.

Chariots and Mobility

Chariots were the cutting-edge military vehicles of their time. First introduced by the Shang, these two-wheeled, horse-drawn platforms allowed warriors to move rapidly across the battlefield while maintaining an elevated position. A typical crew consisted of a driver, an archer, and a spear-wielder. This configuration allowed for mobile archery, quick charges, and controlled retreats.

In battle, chariots were used to harass enemy formations, flank infantry, or provide a platform for elite fighters. They weren't tanks—they were fast, fragile, and depended on flat terrain—but they were devastating in the right conditions. Owning a chariot wasn't just a tactical advantage; it was a symbol of nobility and wealth. In many ways, it was the ancient equivalent of commanding a fighter jet.

As warfare became more frequent and less ritualized, however, chariots began to **decline in importance**. The terrain of central China, filled with rivers, mountains, and forests, wasn't ideal for large-scale chariot warfare. Additionally, the growing size of infantry units made the small, elite chariot teams less relevant. By the late Zhou period, large foot soldier formations began dominating the battlefield, supported by archers and light cavalry.

Early Command Structures

Military leadership in the Bronze Age was **clan-based**, often hereditary, and closely tied to noble families. Kings, dukes, or high-ranking lords would personally lead their forces into battle. Their authority came not just from rank but from ritual standing—if a commander lacked ancestral legitimacy, their command could be challenged.

To maintain order on the battlefield, commanders used **visual and auditory signals**—flags, banners, gongs, and especially drums. These allowed communication across the chaos of war. Certain rhythms signaled retreat, attack, regrouping, or flanking. Troops were trained to respond to these sounds as commands.

Hierarchies were also deeply **ritualized**. Officers were expected to follow strict codes of behavior—both in how they fought and how they interacted with subordinates. This wasn't just military discipline; it was a cultural system that reinforced social order. The battlefield was seen as an extension of the court.

Even in war, *who* you were mattered as much as *what* you could do.

The Bronze Age in China wasn't primitive—it was highly structured, symbol-rich, and technologically advanced for its time. Though limited by material constraints, the early Chinese developed a complex system of war that laid the groundwork for the innovations that followed. From chariot wheels to battle drums, they turned bronze into a military language—and the entire region learned to listen.

2.3 Transition to the Warring States

From Ritual Combat to Total War

As the Zhou Dynasty weakened, the old world of ritualized, clan-based warfare began to collapse. In its place rose a brutal new era defined by political chaos, relentless military innovation, and a race for survival. This period—spanning roughly 475 to 221 BCE—is known as the **Warring States** era, and it marked a turning point in Chinese military history. No longer was war a matter of honor and display. It became a contest of strategy, numbers, and statecraft.

Political Fragmentation

The Zhou kings once held symbolic authority over a network of noble families, but by the 8th century BCE, that authority had eroded. Power devolved into the hands of **regional lords**, each ruling their own territories as de facto kings. These states no longer looked to the Zhou court for guidance. They levied their own taxes, minted their own coins, and most importantly—commanded their own armies.

As Zhou authority collapsed, **rival states rose to fill the vacuum**. Seven major players emerged: Qin, Chu, Zhao, Wei, Han, Yan, and Qi. These states were not just larger—they were more centralized, more militarized, and increasingly hostile toward one another. Warfare became the primary method of diplomacy. Treaties were temporary, alliances shifted constantly, and trust was rare.

This created the conditions for an **arms race** unlike anything China had seen before. States began investing heavily in weapons production, fortifications, and military reforms. The goal was no longer just to defend—it was to dominate.

Military Competition

To meet growing military demands, states could no longer rely solely on aristocratic warriors or temporary peasant levies. They needed **large, permanent fighting forces**. This led to the formation of standing armies, many of which were recruited from the general population. In some states, conscription was mandatory. In others, military service offered a path to upward mobility.

With larger armies came the need for **better training and motivation**. Soldiers were drilled in formation tactics, taught to obey complex commands, and rewarded for performance on the battlefield. Some states implemented systems where soldiers earned rank and social standing through courage and effectiveness rather than birth—a radical idea in ancient China.

Deception became a core part of warfare during this time. **Early spycraft** flourished. States used scouts, defectors, double agents, and misinformation campaigns to destabilize their enemies. Battles were no longer won by force alone but by psychological edge. Sun Bin, a famous strategist from this period and descendant of Sun Tzu, famously used a fake retreat and manipulated enemy expectations to win a decisive victory at the Battle of Maling.

Reforms and Innovation

With war becoming the engine of political survival, **military reform became a priority**. States like Qin, under reformers such as Shang Yang, introduced Legalist policies that drastically reorganized military life. These reforms included:

- **Meritocratic promotions**: Officers were selected based on battlefield achievements, not noble status.

- **Strict codes and punishments**: Discipline was enforced with severe penalties for failure or disobedience.

- **Mass mobilization**: The population was reorganized into households responsible for military service, farming, and surveillance of neighbors.

The **rise of professional generals** also reshaped the battlefield. Unlike the hereditary warlords of the Zhou, these commanders were trained, tested, and chosen for their strategic minds. They understood logistics, siegecraft, terrain, and morale. War became a science, not just an art.

States also innovated in weapons and battlefield techniques. Iron replaced bronze, crossbows were standardized, and complex unit formations like fish-scale and goose-wing arrays were developed to outmaneuver opponents.

The Warring States period was brutal, but it was also transformative. It turned ancient Chinese warfare from a ceremonial duty into a systematic machine. The armies grew larger, the strategies sharper, and the stakes higher. By the end of it, only one state—Qin—would remain. And it would use everything learned during this bloody century to build an empire.

Chapter 3: The Warring States and the Age of Reform

3.1 The Seven Powers

China's Great Military Chessboard

By the 5th century BCE, China had fractured into a brutal contest between **seven dominant states**—each one armed, ambitious, and determined to unify the realm under its own banner. This period wasn't just marked by endless warfare, but by an explosion of **military reform, innovation, and tactical thinking**. With no central power left to mediate, survival depended on strength, strategy, and adaptability. These were no longer ritual battles. This was war at an industrial scale.

The Seven Warring States

The "Seven Warring States" were **Qin, Chu, Zhao, Wei, Han, Yan**, and **Qi**. While dozens of smaller powers existed early on, these seven absorbed or eliminated their rivals over time, carving China into military zones in constant flux.

- **Qin** sat in the far west, somewhat isolated by mountains. It was originally seen as a barbarian borderland but grew into the most ruthless and efficient state through Legalist reforms.

- **Chu** in the south had rich resources, a large population, and a diverse military, including strong naval forces and light infantry. However, it often suffered from loose command structure and political instability.

- **Zhao** and **Wei**, located in the north-central plains, were famed for their cavalry and elite foot soldiers, often innovating with battlefield formations and weapons.

- **Han**, the smallest and weakest, was caught between powerful neighbors and relied heavily on defensive strategies.

- **Yan**, in the northeast, struggled with internal reforms but occasionally fielded strong frontier forces against nomadic incursions.

- **Qi**, on the eastern coast, was known for its wealth, philosophical schools, and a well-organized army led by reformers like Sun Bin.

Each state developed a distinct military identity based on **geography**, available resources, and leadership. Some controlled fertile river valleys perfect for agriculture and mass conscription. Others guarded mountain passes, making them hard to invade but equally difficult to expand from. These **geographic constraints shaped strategy** as much as weapons or manpower.

Arms Escalation

As these states competed for dominance, they plunged into an **arms race** that revolutionized Chinese warfare. Bronze was phased out almost entirely, replaced by **cast iron weapons**—cheaper to make, easier to mass produce, and more durable in combat. Swords, spears, and armor became standardized. Armies grew from a few thousand elite warriors to hundreds of thousands of trained soldiers.

Siege warfare evolved rapidly. Towering siege ramps, mobile battering rams, and ladder-based assaults became common in attempts to capture heavily fortified cities. The invention and refinement of the **crossbow** also changed battlefield dynamics. Unlike traditional bows, crossbows could be used with minimal training and delivered deadly force from a distance with great accuracy—especially in formation.

States like Qin and Zhao developed **scaled infantry formations**, where tightly organized units moved and attacked in coordinated waves. These formations focused on discipline and mutual protection, giving them a significant edge in direct engagements. Warfare was no longer a clash of heroes—it was a contest of systems.

Evolution of Generalship

Out of this environment emerged a new kind of military leader—**the professional general**. Rather than nobles who fought for glory, these men were chosen for their strategic insight and their ability to manage massive forces in complex conditions.

Wu Qi, for example, implemented strict military discipline and emphasized equality among ranks. He punished even minor disobedience and expected generals to eat and sleep like their troops. His reforms made armies leaner, faster, and more loyal.

Sun Bin, a descendant of Sun Tzu, took warfare to a cerebral level. At the Battle of Maling, he tricked his opponent into attacking a seemingly weakened force, only to ambush them in a narrow valley with devastating results. His legacy lives on in the principles of deception, timing, and manipulation that still define strategic thinking today.

Tactical **maneuvering** replaced brute-force engagement. Generals learned to **encircle**, **feint**, **cut supply lines**, and **exploit terrain**. The battlefield became a chessboard, and only those who mastered the long game survived.

The Warring States period was the crucible that forged China's first true military minds and modernized the art of war. It was brutal, brilliant, and transformative—laying the foundation for the empire that would soon rise from the ashes of constant conflict.

3.2 Qin's Military Advantage

How Ruthless Reforms Built an Unstoppable War Machine

By the late Warring States period, **Qin** had transformed from an underestimated frontier state into a rising powerhouse with unmatched military efficiency. While other kingdoms clung to traditions of aristocracy and honor, Qin embraced **Legalist philosophy** and brutal pragmatism. The result was a highly disciplined, well-organized war machine built for conquest. Much of this transformation can be traced to a single man—**Shang Yang**.

Shang Yang's Reforms

Shang Yang was a Legalist reformer who served in the Qin court during the 4th century BCE. His policies were radical, authoritarian, and deeply effective. At the heart of his agenda was the **Legalist military structure**, which prioritized the strength of the state above all else. The military was not a noble privilege—it was a public obligation and a state-run institution.

One of Shang Yang's boldest moves was eliminating the **aristocratic chain of command**. No longer were generals chosen by family status. Promotions were earned strictly through performance. Soldiers who killed a set number of enemies or captured important positions could rise in rank, regardless of background. This **merit-over-bloodline** policy meant that even a peasant could become a general, as long as he proved himself in battle.

To enforce discipline, Shang Yang implemented **harsh penalties** for disobedience, cowardice, or failure to follow orders. If a soldier retreated without command, the entire unit could be punished. While extreme, this approach created ironclad cohesion. Qin soldiers obeyed orders without hesitation—not just from loyalty, but from fear of the consequences.

Mass Conscription

The backbone of Qin's army was its **mass mobilization system**. Unlike other states that relied on seasonal levies or volunteer forces, Qin treated warfare as a year-round national duty.

A population **census** was conducted to track every household. Based on this data, the state could draft soldiers in waves and organize them according to age, skill, and geographic origin. The **peasant-soldier system** turned farmers into warriors. Men would serve for a period, return to tend their land, then rotate back into military service as needed.

This system had several advantages. It ensured a **constant supply of manpower**, kept soldiers tied to their communities, and integrated military training into daily life. It also blurred the line between civilian and soldier, strengthening the sense of national unity and sacrifice.

Qin's **rotational service model** meant that even during peacetime, soldiers were available for defense, construction, or rapid deployment. There were no long gaps between wars—every man was either fighting, preparing to fight, or supporting those who were.

Technological Superiority

Qin's military dominance wasn't just about manpower—it was also about tools, infrastructure, and foresight.

First, Qin **standardized cast iron weapons**. Spearheads, swords, armor plates, and arrowheads were produced in large quantities using molds. This allowed for quicker replacement, uniform quality, and easier logistics in outfitting troops. Standardization also extended to weight systems, road widths, and even cart axle sizes—ensuring that supply wagons and weapons fit across the empire.

The **road network** Qin built was arguably as important as its army. Straight, wide, and stone-paved, these roads connected the capital to border garrisons, making troop movements faster and more reliable than in any other state. Supplies could be moved quickly, reinforcements deployed with precision, and injured soldiers evacuated efficiently.

Qin also developed **early military logistics systems**, including granaries placed along campaign routes, signal towers for rapid communication, and rest stations for messengers and scouts. These systems allowed generals to plan multi-stage operations and sustain long campaigns without relying on looting or unreliable foraging.

Qin didn't just win because it fought harder—it won because it **fought smarter**. With a brutal legal framework, a professionalized army, and a logistical backbone that rivaled anything of its time, Qin was uniquely positioned to outlast and overpower its rivals. By turning the entire state into a war engine, it laid the groundwork for the first unified Chinese empire—and a new chapter in the art of war.

3.3 The Final Conquests

The Fall of Rivals and the Birth of Empire

By the late third century BCE, the chessboard of the Warring States was almost cleared. Most of the minor players had been eliminated, and the remaining kingdoms—Zhao, Chu, Yan, and Qi—were bracing for Qin's advance. While each had once been powerful in its own right, Qin's relentless military reforms and ruthless strategies had made it nearly unstoppable. Still, the final victories did not come without fierce resistance, clever deception, and calculated brutality.

Zhao and the Elite Cavalry

Among Qin's last serious rivals was the state of **Zhao**, known for its powerful **elite cavalry** and skilled commanders. Facing threats from both Qin and nomadic groups to the north, Zhao had developed a flexible, fast-moving army capable of operating across difficult terrain. This included adoption of the **"Wuhu" horse archer** tactics—named after the nomadic tribes they often fought—who favored hit-and-run strikes, composite bows, and guerrilla-style warfare.

Zhao's **frontier defense system** relied heavily on fortified passes, river boundaries, and mounted patrols. However, while it had strong individual units and capable generals like Li Mu, Zhao lacked the centralized coordination and deep logistical support that Qin had mastered.

In 228 BCE, Qin launched its decisive assault. The elite cavalry of Zhao, stretched thin and outmaneuvered, couldn't hold the line. After a series of brutal skirmishes, Qin forces pushed deep into Zhao territory, capturing its capital **Handan**, once considered nearly impregnable.

Siege of Handan and Deception

The **Siege of Handan** revealed another layer of Qin's dominance: psychological warfare. The Qin leadership, under General Wang Jian and others, didn't rely solely on brute force. They used **bribery, misinformation, and manipulation** to weaken enemy morale and split alliances before battles even began.

In Handan, rumors were deliberately spread to convince citizens that their leaders had already fled. Qin spies paid off officials to sabotage defenses, delay reinforcements, and turn public sentiment against the defenders. Even Zhao's elite cavalry couldn't save a city that was breaking from within.

This siege was emblematic of Qin's broader strategy. Rather than fighting every army head-on, it **broke coalitions**, **turned allies into enemies**, and **undermined willpower**. Qin understood that winning a war often started long before the battlefield.

Unification Under Qin

The fall of Zhao marked the beginning of the end. In the years that followed, **Qin launched final campaigns** against Yan, Wei, Chu, and Qi—each more vulnerable than the last. Some surrendered with barely a fight. Others, like Chu, resisted bitterly, only to be crushed by Qin's superior organization and supply chains.

Central to these victories was **General Wang Jian**, one of Qin's most experienced and cautious commanders. Unlike hot-headed rivals, Wang Jian preferred slow, methodical progress. In the massive invasion of Chu, he demanded a huge army and refused to act rashly. His patience paid off—Chu's much larger force was eventually outmaneuvered, outlasted, and broken.

By 221 BCE, the last holdout—Qi—submitted. **Qin had achieved what no state before it had accomplished: the full military unification of China.** The ruler of Qin, King Zheng, declared himself **Qin Shi Huang**, the First Emperor. With this, the Warring States era ended—and the imperial age began.

Qin's conquests weren't inevitable. They were earned through superior planning, ruthless efficiency, and a willingness to embrace innovation where others clung to tradition. By mastering not just the battlefield but also the psychological and political dimensions of war, Qin didn't just defeat its enemies—it dismantled the entire Warring States system.

The empire was born in blood, iron, and ambition—and its legacy would shape China for millennia to come.

Chapter 4: The Qin Dynasty and Total War

4.1 Rise of a Centralized Army

How Qin Turned War Into Statecraft

The unification of China under the **Qin Dynasty** was not simply a military triumph—it was a political revolution. Where other states had relied on hereditary warlords and feudal command structures, Qin replaced tradition with efficiency. Under the rule of **Qin Shi Huang**, warfare became fully integrated into state administration. The army was no longer an extension of noble households—it was an arm of the emperor himself.

Abolishment of Noble-Led Forces

One of the first actions Qin took after consolidation was the **elimination of independent military power**. During the Warring States period, nobles often maintained personal armies, loyal only to their clans or regions. This made central control fragile, and rebellions frequent.

Qin changed this by **abolishing noble-led forces altogether**. All military authority was stripped from hereditary lords, and local militias were either absorbed or disbanded. In their place, the Qin created a **national standing army**—organized, salaried, and loyal only to the emperor.

To prevent the rise of regional power bases, Qin also **replaced feudal lords with appointed governors**. These governors had administrative and military responsibilities but were rotated regularly and kept under close surveillance. The new **centralized command structure** allowed orders to flow directly from the capital to the front lines, cutting down on delays, confusion, and betrayal.

This highly disciplined, unified approach became a cornerstone of the Qin military advantage. Authority was clear, obedience was non-negotiable, and control was absolute.

Standardization

What made the Qin army so effective wasn't just discipline—it was **uniformity**. The state undertook massive efforts to **standardize weapons**, making them easier to produce, repair, and distribute. Spears, swords, crossbows, arrowheads, and armor were cast using identical molds, ensuring consistent quality and compatibility. If a soldier lost a blade, it could be replaced instantly from any armory in the empire.

Beyond weaponry, **standardization extended to logistics**: measurement units, axle widths, coinage, and written scripts were all unified. This streamlined transportation, communication, and coordination across vast territories.

Qin also enforced **universal conscription**. Every eligible male was expected to serve the state—either in the military or in public works projects like road building or wall construction. This not only guaranteed a steady stream of soldiers but also reinforced the belief that every citizen was bound to the state by duty.

A strict **code of military conduct** governed behavior in and out of battle. Rewards were given for bravery, promotions earned by merit, and harsh punishments delivered for cowardice or disobedience. Soldiers were expected to report infractions and follow commands without question. It was a cold system—but it worked.

Infrastructure for War

Unlike earlier dynasties that waged war and went home, the Qin prepared for **perpetual readiness**. Warfare was not an event—it was an ongoing state of preparedness built into the very geography of the empire.

One of their boldest projects was the early **construction of the Great Wall**. While not the continuous structure seen today, this wall was a network of **fortifications, watchtowers, and defensive outposts**, meant to protect the northern frontier from nomadic incursions. Qin connected and expanded existing walls, creating the first large-scale border defense system.

Qin also built a vast system of **military roads**—straight, paved, and maintained by the state. These roads allowed for the rapid movement of troops, messengers, and supplies. Alongside them were **supply depots**, water sources, and rest stations, forming the backbone of Qin's **military logistics network**.

Finally, **fortified borders** were established across key chokepoints. These outposts weren't just for defense—they were symbols of Qin control, psychological markers that reminded both citizens and enemies of the empire's reach.

With its centralized command, uniform weaponry, and infrastructure-first approach, the Qin Dynasty turned war into a system—ruthless, efficient, and terrifyingly effective. In doing so, it laid the foundations not just for empire, but for the way China would organize military power for centuries to come.

4.2 The Campaigns of Conquest

How Qin Crushed Resistance and Engineered an Empire

Once Qin had transformed its military into a centralized war machine, it turned that force outward to **finish what centuries of war had begun**—the unification of China. With states like **Chu** and **Qi** still standing, the Qin court launched its final campaigns with overwhelming strength and brutal precision. These were not simply battles. They were military occupations backed by surveillance, suppression, and large-scale engineering projects designed to reshape geography, not just politics.

Against Chu and Qi

Chu was Qin's most serious remaining rival. Large, resource-rich, and located in the south, Chu had once been a military powerhouse. But internal divisions and inconsistent leadership left it vulnerable by the time Qin attacked.

The invasion was led by **General Wang Jian**, who insisted on deploying an enormous army—estimated at **600,000 troops**. While some advisors mocked his caution, it proved to be wise. Chu's armies were scattered, and Wang Jian used **careful logistics, deliberate pacing,** and surprise maneuvers to wear them down. Key victories came through **river crossings**, where Qin troops used portable bridges and feints to draw out Chu defenders, then **launched ambushes** on retreating forces.

When Chu was defeated, the Qin response was swift: generals and noble families were executed, populations were resettled, and local governance was replaced by Qin administrators. **Qi**, on the other hand, surrendered almost without resistance. Recognizing the futility of war, Qi's leadership negotiated peaceful absorption—though Qin still deployed troops to ensure compliance.

Qin's post-victory policy was one of **integration by force**. Surrendered regions were quickly absorbed into the Qin administrative system, their cultures rebranded, and their loyalties tested under the threat of execution.

Internal Suppression

Conquest didn't mean peace. Qin faced constant internal instability, especially in newly annexed territories. Rather than relying on leniency, the regime doubled down on **harsh suppression**. Rebellions were met with **mass executions**, often wiping out not only rebels but their extended families. The goal was deterrence through fear.

Even Qin's own commanders weren't safe. The court maintained an elaborate system of **surveillance over generals**, using spies, informants, and court officials to monitor loyalty. Generals who became too popular or hesitant were recalled, demoted, or executed. This constant oversight ensured obedience but created a climate of anxiety among Qin's leadership class.

Still, the strategy was effective. Local uprisings were crushed before they could spread. Roads and communication towers allowed for **rapid military response**, and mass deportations disrupted potential rebellions by splitting up communities.

Engineering as Warfare

Qin didn't rely solely on the sword to win battles. It also turned to engineering—**using the landscape itself as a weapon**.

- In flood-prone regions, Qin forces constructed **canals and redirected rivers** to destroy enemy defenses or force populations into submission. These **flood traps** could wipe out garrisons or isolate cities without a single sword being drawn.

- When capturing cities, Qin often **dismantled existing fortifications** stone by stone, preventing future resistance. Recycled materials were used to build roads or walls elsewhere, turning conquered cities into supply depots.

- In forested areas, Qin troops practiced **strategic deforestation**—cutting down trees not only to deny cover to enemy troops, but to clear paths for roads and prevent ambushes. Forests were also burned to displace local populations and destroy rebel hideouts.

These engineering tactics weren't just practical—they were psychological. They demonstrated that Qin could shape nature itself to enforce its will.

The final Qin campaigns were more than military operations. They were acts of **total control**, blending battlefield dominance with fear, surveillance, and environmental manipulation. Qin didn't just defeat its enemies—it erased their ability to resist, reshaped their homelands, and embedded its rule in both stone and soil.

In the next chapter, we'll explore how this relentless expansion would eventually turn inward—and how the very tools Qin used to build an empire would also fuel its downfall.

4.3 Fall of the Qin

How the Empire That Conquered All Collapsed From Within

The Qin Dynasty's rise was swift and absolute. In less than two decades, it had unified China through unmatched military force, political centralization, and legalist discipline. But that same speed—its strength in war—became its weakness in peace. The Qin did not fall to foreign invaders or rival states. It collapsed under the weight of its own success.

Overextension

At its height, Qin controlled more territory than any Chinese state before it. But **conquering land is not the same as governing it**. The empire stretched across diverse regions—mountains, deserts, rivers, and cities—with different cultures, languages, and loyalties. Qin's centralized system, designed for control, was overwhelmed by the need to administer it all.

- **Resources were stretched thin**, especially with the need to maintain garrisons, build walls, and supply soldiers across vast distances.

- Troops, **exhausted from constant campaigning**, were kept in rotation with little rest. Morale dropped. Loyalty wavered.

- The burden fell hardest on the people. Taxes increased. Forced labor expanded. Citizens who once welcomed Qin rule now felt **trapped by it**.

Even the infrastructure that had enabled conquest—roads, canals, and walls—became a source of tension. Massive construction projects drained the treasury and demanded backbreaking labor. This generated **popular unrest** on a national scale.

Peasant Rebellions

The breaking point came not from a rival state, but from a **pair of low-ranking officers: Chen Sheng and Wu Guang**. In 209 BCE, they were ordered to transport troops to a frontier post. Bad weather delayed them, and they faced execution for arriving late—a typical Qin punishment. Rather than submit, they **rebelled**.

Their uprising began with a few hundred followers, but it ignited a spark across the empire. **Discontented veterans**, oppressed peasants, and even local elites joined in. The rebellion exposed the deep **resentment beneath the surface** of Qin rule.

What terrified the Qin court wasn't just the rebellion itself—it was **how fast it spread**. Without strong local leaders to counter it (thanks to Qin's policy of rotating governors), and with troops too scattered to respond quickly, the central government **lost control of its own empire**.

The Qin response was predictably harsh—mass executions, new laws, tighter restrictions—but these only accelerated the collapse.

The Death of a Dynasty

Qin Shi Huang, the First Emperor, died in 210 BCE during an inspection tour. His death was covered up by court officials who manipulated his will and installed a weaker successor—his son, **Qin Er Shi**, who lacked both charisma and authority.

With no legitimate leadership, and with enemies on every front, the government fractured. Rebellions multiplied. Even loyal generals questioned the regime's ability to survive.

By 206 BCE, just 15 years after its founding, the Qin Dynasty was gone. Its capital was captured. The imperial line was extinguished. The empire it had built was divided once again.

Lessons in Leadership Failure

The Qin Dynasty's collapse offers a powerful lesson: **military strength alone is not enough to sustain an empire**.

- The Qin failed to adapt to peacetime governance. What worked during conquest—strict laws, fear, absolute centralization—bred resentment once victory was achieved.

- The state ignored the needs of its soldiers and citizens. Veterans went unpaid, laborers were pushed to the brink, and dissent was crushed rather than addressed.

- Leadership succession was mishandled. With no capable ruler to follow Qin Shi Huang, the empire lacked vision, stability, and flexibility.

Ultimately, the Qin dynasty conquered China but **never earned its trust**. It ruled through fear and efficiency, but not through legitimacy or connection. Its fall marked not just the end of a regime, but the end of an experiment in total control.

Chapter 5: Han Dynasty—Tactics of a Rising Empire

5.1 Rebuilding the Army

From Rebellion to Reform: How the Han Reforged China's Military

After the collapse of the Qin Dynasty, China was once again in chaos. Warlords scrambled for power, and the centralized machinery of the state disintegrated. In this unstable vacuum emerged an unlikely figure—**Liu Bang**, a former peasant and low-ranking official, who would eventually become **Emperor Gaozu**, founder of the **Han Dynasty**. His rise marked not just a political shift, but a critical moment in the evolution of Chinese warfare. The Han didn't just inherit Qin's army—they reimagined it.

From Rebels to Rulers

Liu Bang was not a traditional military genius. In fact, he won his earliest battles more through **charisma and diplomacy** than battlefield prowess. He gained support by treating civilians and prisoners with respect—something the Qin had rarely done. He also **recruited defected generals**, many of whom had once served the Qin or rival warlords, and offered them positions in exchange for loyalty.

This strategy allowed Liu Bang to **turn chaos into order**. Instead of dismantling the military structures left behind by the Qin, he co-opted and modified them. He understood that controlling China meant more than just seizing cities. It required securing roads, rebuilding supply lines, and organizing soldiers under a system people could trust.

One of Liu Bang's greatest strengths was knowing what to keep and what to discard. He kept Qin's logistical frameworks, such as their road system and conscription model, but **softened their authoritarian edge**. He began to shift military service from a state of fear to a state of responsibility.

Creation of a Professional Force

Under the Han, the military evolved from a reactive force into a long-term institution. The state introduced **formal command hierarchies**, where roles were clearly defined and officers were expected to lead by example. Generals were no longer feared as potential rivals (as they had been under the Qin), but integrated into the broader system of governance.

Soldiers were assigned **long-term service roles**, often alternating between active duty and civilian life. This kept them trained and available while reducing the social disruption of full-time military life. Veterans received land or positions in government service, creating a sense of career progression and loyalty.

The Han also laid the foundation for **military academies**—structured places of learning where future officers were trained not only in tactics and martial arts, but also in logistics, philosophy, and Confucian ethics. Education became a cornerstone of leadership. An ideal general was expected to be disciplined, strategic, and morally upright.

This was a key departure from Qin Legalism. Rather than rewarding only results, the Han emphasized character and integrity alongside effectiveness.

Balancing Civil and Military Power

While the Han valued a strong army, it also feared the dangers of military overreach. Qin had collapsed partly because its generals became too powerful—or too distrusted. To avoid repeating that mistake, the Han introduced **a system of civilian oversight** over military affairs.

Civil officials monitored troop movements, audited supply chains, and reported directly to the emperor. Generals were expected to consult with civilian advisors and justify their decisions through proper channels. This dual structure imposed **bureaucratic checks** on the use of force, reinforcing the emperor's control while preventing insubordination.

This reflected a deeper **Confucian restraint**. Warfare, though necessary, was not to be glorified. The ideal state was peaceful, ordered, and moral. Military action had to be justified as a tool of defense, not ambition. Aggression for its own sake was frowned upon, and generals who defied these values could be recalled, demoted, or even executed.

The early Han military wasn't just a continuation of Qin tactics—it was a reform of Qin's entire philosophy. By blending strategic efficiency with ethical governance, the Han laid the groundwork for an army that could not only fight, but endure. And in doing so, they built one of the most resilient empires in Chinese history.

5.2 Expansion and Diplomacy

How the Han Balanced Conquest With Control

Once the Han Dynasty stabilized its core territory, it looked outward—not just to expand, but to secure its borders, trade routes, and influence. Unlike the Qin, whose power was rooted in internal suppression, the Han recognized that endurance required **both force and flexibility**. This chapter explores how Han leaders fought wars of necessity and diplomacy in three directions: the **northern steppes**, the **western trade routes**, and the **southern frontiers**.

Han–Xiongnu Wars

The most persistent threat to early Han security came from the **Xiongnu**, a confederation of nomadic tribes from the northern steppes. These fierce horse archers specialized in **hit-and-run raids**, appearing and vanishing across vast, open terrain where infantry struggled to follow. Han infantry, trained for field battles and city defense, was at a disadvantage.

The Han had to adapt. The government created a hybrid force—**cavalry units trained in nomadic tactics** and supported by fortified supply lines. Still, the **harsh terrain** and unpredictable **weather** of the steppes often slowed campaigns. Summer dust storms, freezing winters, and sparse water sources meant that **logistics mattered as much as combat**.

Rather than fight an endless war, Emperor Wu of Han launched a long-term **frontier strategy**. This included building **border garrisons**, establishing outposts deep into steppe territory, and resettling loyal groups as buffers between China and the Xiongnu. The aim wasn't immediate victory—it was containment, deterrence, and slow erosion of Xiongnu unity.

Silk Road Defense

As Han influence grew westward, it opened what would become the **Silk Road**—a trade network connecting China to Central Asia, Persia, and beyond. This wasn't just about luxury goods. It was about projecting power and ensuring economic lifelines.

To protect these trade corridors, the Han built **fortified garrisons along key routes** in Gansu and the Tarim Basin. These outposts housed troops, traders, and officials. They also served as rest stops for caravans and resupply points for military patrols.

Diplomacy played a critical role. The Han made **alliances with Central Asian tribes**, offering protection, marriage ties, and trade incentives. At times, military force backed these deals. When local leaders resisted, the Han responded with swift campaigns to enforce cooperation.

This combination of **diplomatic outreach and military presence** allowed the Han to secure vast stretches of land with fewer soldiers than outright conquest would require. It also gave the empire a reputation as a power willing to negotiate—but capable of punishment when necessary.

Han in the South

The Han didn't just expand north and west—they also moved south into what is now southern China and northern Vietnam. These areas were rich in resources but populated by **diverse tribal groups** who had their own languages, customs, and forms of resistance.

To conquer these regions, the Han relied heavily on **river and coastal warfare**. Naval technology advanced with **flat-bottom boats**, better suited to shallow waters, and **paddlewheel propulsion**, which improved maneuverability. These innovations allowed the Han to push deep into **tropical river systems**, turning **waterways into battlefields**.

Once conquered, the southern regions were not simply ruled—they were **assimilated**. Han authorities promoted Chinese customs, established schools, and built roads and canals. Tribal leaders were offered positions in the imperial system, blending diplomacy with control.

But this process wasn't smooth. Rebellions were frequent, especially in the early stages. The Han often had to **re-invade areas multiple times**, reminding locals that peace came at the price of submission.

The Han Dynasty succeeded where the Qin failed because it **adapted to its borders**. It didn't treat every enemy the same. Against nomads, it built strongholds and used cavalry. In the west, it mixed diplomacy with protection. In the south, it combined naval power with cultural absorption. Expansion was not just about territory—it was about building **a strategic framework that could survive war, trade, and time**.

5.3 Military Innovations

Weapons, Mobility, and the Engine Behind the Han War Machine

To maintain and expand an empire the size of Han China, military might alone wasn't enough. Victory required innovation—tools and tactics that gave the Han army speed, endurance, and control across thousands of miles. From **repeating crossbows** to **horse-mounted archery** and **logistical engineering**, the Han military system became one of the most advanced in the ancient world.

Repeating Crossbows

Among the most famous Han inventions was the **repeating crossbow**—a mechanical leap forward in ranged weaponry. Traditional crossbows, while powerful and accurate, required careful loading and winding after each shot. In contrast, the repeating model featured a lever-and-magazine mechanism that allowed soldiers to fire multiple bolts in quick succession with one hand motion.

This improvement boosted both **range and reload efficiency**, making it ideal for **defensive formations, ambushes, and urban warfare**. Infantry could unleash sustained volleys against advancing enemies with minimal training. It wasn't as powerful as a single-shot crossbow, but its ease of use and speed made it invaluable, especially when deployed in large numbers.

Compared to earlier Zhou and Warring States crossbows, the Han models were more **compact, reliable, and mass-produced**, thanks to standardized iron parts and state-managed workshops. In a time when terrain and troop morale often decided engagements, having units that could hold off attackers with rapid, consistent fire provided a major tactical advantage.

Horse-Mounted Archery

Facing constant pressure from the Xiongnu and other nomadic tribes, the Han military was forced to rethink its traditional infantry-based doctrine. The response was clear: **adopt what works, even if it comes from your enemy**.

The Han began training their own **horse-mounted archers**, combining **mobility, range, and speed** into a new kind of strike force. These soldiers were taught to ride and shoot simultaneously, a skill that required years of practice and specialized equipment like recurved bows, lightweight armor, and stirrup-like foot holds.

To support this shift, the Han established **new training systems**, often in frontier garrisons where recruits lived under direct supervision and practiced year-round. They also created **cavalry divisions** dedicated to rapid response, patrolling borderlands and intercepting raiders before they reached settled areas.

This transformation marked a broader recognition: **mobility was now as important as numbers**. Cavalry units weren't just support—they were becoming central to battlefield success.

Logistics and Supply Chains

Behind every victory was an engine of planning. The Han understood that an army marches not just on discipline but on **food, gear, and fuel**.

The government developed extensive **warehouse and granary systems**, strategically placed along military roads, rivers, and trade routes. These stores ensured that soldiers had consistent access to grain, dried meat, and water—essential in long campaigns where foraging could not be relied upon.

River transport became a central feature of military logistics. The Han built canals and improved navigability in major waterways, allowing entire armies to move with speed and supplies. Barges carried food, weapons, and reinforcements downstream toward the front, reducing reliance on slow overland convoys.

To secure these routes, the Han employed **route protection strategies**: stationed troops along bridges and passes, constructed rest stops for couriers, and set up beacon towers for emergency signaling. These measures allowed generals to plan months ahead, knowing exactly how and when supplies would arrive.

Through innovation in weaponry, adoption of foreign tactics, and the construction of an efficient support network, the Han Dynasty transformed warfare from episodic confrontation into a system of **sustained, state-backed dominance**. Their armies didn't just win—they endured. And in doing so, they laid the blueprint for how China would conduct war for centuries to come.

Chapter 6: Three Kingdoms—Warlords and Master Strategists

6.1 The Collapse of Han

From Imperial Decline to Warlord Dominance

The Han Dynasty, once a symbol of unity and innovation, did not fall in a single battle—it unraveled from within. By the end of the 2nd century CE, the empire had become a hollow shell, its institutions rotting from court corruption, military factionalism, and rural chaos. This vacuum of power set the stage for one of China's most turbulent and legendary periods: the **Three Kingdoms era**.

Fragmentation of Power

The decline of Han authority began at the very top. In the final decades of the dynasty, emperors were little more than puppets, manipulated by **eunuchs and court officials** who vied for influence. These eunuchs not only controlled access to the throne but also diverted military funding and undermined loyal generals.

As central power weakened, **regional commanders and governors**—initially loyal defenders of the realm—began carving out their own territories. With the capital's authority in question, these men stopped following imperial orders and started acting as independent rulers. Many raised their own armies, imposed local taxes, and prepared for inevitable confrontation.

Meanwhile, discontent among the people reached a breaking point. Natural disasters, heavy taxation, and mismanagement led to a wave of **peasant rebellions**, most notably the **Yellow Turban Uprising** in 184 CE. Though the rebellion was eventually crushed, it **reignited warfare across the empire**. Warlords who had fought side-by-side against the rebels soon turned on each other.

The Han state survived in name, but its structure had collapsed. China was now a chessboard of warlords—each claiming legitimacy, each vying for dominance.

Rise of Cao Cao

In the midst of this chaos emerged **Cao Cao**, one of the most controversial and brilliant figures in Chinese history. Originally a minor official, he rose quickly through both **military success and political cunning**. His early campaigns focused on stabilizing northern China, restoring law and order in regions devastated by rebellion and lawlessness.

Cao Cao's strength wasn't just battlefield skill—it was **strategy and manipulation**. He built a strong power base in the north by rewarding loyal officers and intimidating rivals. He offered protection to commoners while crushing resistance with calculated brutality. His mix of **fear and loyalty** created a dependable war machine and a formidable state: **Wei**.

Under Cao Cao, the Wei state maintained order through conscription, land reforms, and propaganda. Soldiers served in rotation while farming lands granted by the state. This system allowed Cao Cao to sustain large armies without exhausting his resources.

He also **recruited talent based on ability**, not rank. Many of his generals and advisors came from humble backgrounds, united by loyalty and merit. In a fractured world, Cao Cao offered structure—and many flocked to his banner.

Sun Quan and Liu Bei

To the south, two more powers began to rise: **Sun Quan**, ruler of **Wu**, and **Liu Bei**, founder of **Shu Han**. Both would become legendary figures in their own right, not just for their military roles but for their contrasting visions of leadership.

Sun Quan's strength came from the rivers. His forces mastered **naval warfare**, using swift, maneuverable boats to dominate the Yangtze and protect Wu's southern borders. Under Sun's rule, Wu became a stable, maritime-focused state with a strong economy and elite coastal defenses.

Liu Bei, by contrast, built his state through **alliances and idealism**. Claiming descent from the Han imperial family, he positioned himself as the legitimate heir to a fallen dynasty. Through diplomacy and personal charisma, he attracted allies like the brilliant strategist **Zhuge Liang**, and formed a base in the western regions.

The result was the creation of **Shu Han**, a state built less on military conquest and more on loyalty, honor, and moral legitimacy. In Liu Bei, many saw the restoration of the Han spirit—even if he lacked the resources of his rivals.

The collapse of Han was not an end but a transformation. In its ashes rose three competing visions for China's future—militarized realism, naval independence, and idealistic revival. The wars between these kingdoms would shape not only military history, but China's cultural imagination for centuries.

6.2 Iconic Battles

Turning Points That Redefined Warfare in the Three Kingdoms Era

In a time dominated by rival warlords, strategy mattered more than sheer numbers. The Three Kingdoms period gave rise to some of the most iconic and well-documented battles in Chinese history. These were clashes where generals outwitted enemies through deception, where geography played as large a role as armies, and where decisions made in moments altered the balance of power for years to come.

The Battle of Guandu (200 CE)

The first major turning point came at **Guandu**, a confrontation between the rising force of **Cao Cao** and the dominant northern warlord **Yuan Shao**. On paper, Yuan had every advantage: more troops, more supplies, and a larger territory. But Cao Cao had two key assets—**superior strategy** and **a deep understanding of psychological warfare**.

Knowing he couldn't win in a frontal assault, Cao Cao employed a series of **deception tactics**. He **launched surprise raids on Yuan's supply lines**, forcing the enemy to retreat despite holding superior ground. Yuan's inability to respond decisively, coupled with internal dissent in his camp, led to his **collapse**—a shocking defeat that eliminated the greatest threat to Cao Cao's control of northern China.

What made Guandu so influential wasn't the scale of the battle, but the **lesson in patience and precision**. Cao Cao didn't rush into conflict; he waited, observed, and struck at weaknesses others couldn't see. This battle secured the north for the emerging Wei state.

The Battle of Red Cliffs (208–209 CE)

Perhaps the most famous battle of the era, **Red Cliffs** was a stunning reversal of power. After uniting much of the north, Cao Cao marched south with a massive fleet to crush the alliance of **Sun Quan and Liu Bei**. His goal: complete unification of China under Wei.

But the south had different plans.

The southern coalition, advised by **Zhou Yu** and **Zhuge Liang**, turned the terrain and climate into weapons. Cao Cao's fleet, comprised mostly of **northern troops unfamiliar with river warfare**, was vulnerable. The southern forces launched a **fire attack**, exploiting the wind direction and **burning Cao Cao's ships**, which were lashed together and unable to maneuver.

Weather and timing proved decisive. The allied forces also employed **feigned defections** and **naval formations** that lured Cao Cao into a false sense of security. The result was catastrophic for Wei—thousands of soldiers perished, and the campaign ended in retreat.

Red Cliffs wasn't just a military defeat—it was a **strategic shift**. It ensured the survival of Wu and Shu Han, dividing China into three kingdoms and preventing northern dominance. It also showcased the power of **coalition warfare**, where rival states temporarily united for mutual survival.

Hanzhong Campaign (217–219 CE)

In the rugged mountains of **Hanzhong**, **Liu Bei** faced off against **Cao Cao** in a campaign that would decide control of the western frontier. Unlike Guandu or Red Cliffs, this was a prolonged struggle of attrition, featuring **mountain warfare, ambushes, and sieges**.

Liu Bei, aided by **Fa Zheng** and **Huang Zhong**, used terrain to his advantage. He employed **guerrilla tactics**, cut off supply routes, and **used deceptive positioning** to force Cao Cao's withdrawal. The campaign also featured **psychological manipulation**, including mock retreats and rumors to sow fear among enemy troops.

Crucially, Liu Bei's forces **avoided full confrontation** until their position was secure. They used **tactical retreats** not as signs of weakness, but as strategic moves to wear down the enemy. When victory finally came, Liu Bei declared himself ruler of **Shu Han**, cementing his legitimacy as a rival emperor.

These three battles—**Guandu, Red Cliffs**, and **Hanzhong**—weren't just clashes of arms. They were masterclasses in strategy, adaptation, and leadership. They showed that in times of chaos, victory didn't belong to the strongest army, but to the **most disciplined minds** and **flexible tactics**.

6.3 Zhuge Liang's Legacy

The Sage Who Waged War With Wisdom—and Warnings

Of all the figures to emerge from the Three Kingdoms period, **Zhuge Liang**, the famed chancellor of Shu Han, stands apart. Celebrated not for brute strength but for his intellect, Zhuge Liang became a symbol of **scholarly warfare**, blending Confucian ethics with battlefield innovation. Yet his legacy is not without complications. His genius was real—but so were the limits of strategy when faced with harsh realities.

Strategy Through Adaptation

Zhuge Liang's most famous campaigns weren't victories—they were lessons in persistence, adaptability, and discipline. Tasked with leading **Shu Han's northern expeditions** against the powerful state of Wei, he faced a daunting mix of challenges: inferior troop numbers, mountainous terrain, and a populace weary of prolonged war.

Rather than force decisive battles, Zhuge Liang focused on **logistics, morale, and steady pressure**. His **southern campaigns**—against rebellious tribes in what is now Yunnan and Guizhou—became a model for **using diplomacy alongside force**. He pacified the south not just with arms, but with incentives, infrastructure, and respect for local customs.

In the north, he was a master of **terrain management**, often using defensive positions, supply chains, and **psychological tactics** to outlast his opponents. The most famous example: the **"Empty Fort Strategy"**, where he bluffed an incoming enemy by sitting calmly in an open city, playing a zither. The enemy, suspecting a trap, withdrew. It was pure mind game—a gamble, but one only a master strategist could pull off.

Zhuge Liang showed that sometimes, **not fighting is the ultimate form of warfare**.

Inventions and Tools

Though remembered as a strategist, Zhuge Liang also left his mark through **practical military innovations**.

- He devised the **wooden ox and flowing horse**, wheelbarrow-like carts that improved **supply transport** over rugged terrain. These helped Shu troops carry food and equipment through narrow mountain passes—critical for long campaigns with limited local resources.

- He introduced improvements to **directional arrows** and crossbow mechanisms, enhancing precision and consistency in infantry volleys.

- On the battlefield, he emphasized **communication systems**—including **flag-based signaling and drum codes**—that allowed Shu commanders to coordinate over large distances or in chaotic terrain.

These tools didn't win wars on their own, but they reflect a key part of Zhuge Liang's thinking: **every problem had a technical or tactical solution**—if one was patient and prepared.

Death and Decline

Despite his brilliance, Zhuge Liang's final years were marked by **exhaustion, failure, and disillusionment**. His repeated campaigns into the north drained Shu's manpower and strained its economy. Troops grew tired. Food became scarce. And **alliances—once firm—began to falter**.

He died during his final campaign, succumbing to illness in the field. His army, held together by his presence, **collapsed shortly after**. Without him, Shu lacked leadership with equal vision or authority. His successors couldn't maintain unity or momentum.

Some historians argue Zhuge Liang suffered from **intellectual overreach**—believing that meticulous planning could overcome political weakness and logistical limitations. His loyalty to Shu and to Liu Bei's vision kept him pushing forward, even when the odds said retreat.

But even in failure, his legend only grew. Generals studied his writings. Scholars admired his virtue. His life became a **cautionary tale and a guidebook**—a rare combination in military history.

Zhuge Liang didn't win the war. But he won something more enduring: **respect across centuries**. His legacy reminds us that military power isn't always about conquest. Sometimes, it's about **how long you can hold together an ideal**, even when the world breaks around it.

Chapter 7: Jin and the Age of Decline

7.1 Post-Three Kingdoms Disorder

From Unification to Breakdown: The Jin Dynasty's Struggle to Hold China Together

After decades of bloodshed between Wei, Shu, and Wu, the unification of China under the **Jin Dynasty** in 280 CE should have marked a return to peace. But the reality was far from stable. What followed was not a golden age—but a slow-motion collapse. The Jin may have ended the Three Kingdoms, but they couldn't end the chaos. Instead, they presided over a new era of fragmentation, invasion, and internal decay.

Internal Weakening

The Jin Dynasty inherited the **shell of an empire**, not its soul. Power was concentrated in the hands of a few elite families who treated the state as a personal inheritance. **Corruption flourished**, as ministers and princes competed for favor and influence. Merit was no longer the path to power—bloodline and connections ruled the court.

Succession issues plagued the dynasty almost from the beginning. Emperor Sima Yan, who had unified China, failed to leave behind a strong successor. His son, Sima Zhong, was famously unfit to rule—mentally incapacitated and easily manipulated. This led to the disastrous **War of the Eight Princes**, a civil war among imperial relatives that shattered Jin's credibility and drained its military resources.

With the emperor increasingly sidelined and focused on court intrigues, the **imperial government neglected its provinces**. Taxes went uncollected, garrisons were undersupplied, and roads fell into disrepair. The tools of central control rusted away.

Barbarian Incursions

While the Jin court squabbled, threats from beyond the northern frontier grew bolder. For centuries, the Chinese had managed the **nomadic tribes of the steppes** through a mix of diplomacy, trade, and military deterrence. But with Jin's army weakened and fragmented, these tribes saw opportunity.

This era saw the rise of the so-called **"Five Barbarians"**—a mix of Xiongnu, Jie, Xianbei, Qiang, and Di peoples who began crossing the northern borders not just as raiders, but as **conquerors**. Some had already lived within Chinese territory under previous arrangements. Now, they sensed weakness—and they struck.

Using **cavalry raids**, these nomadic forces bypassed traditional city defenses, struck supply centers, and conducted **massacres** in Chinese heartlands. Whole populations were displaced. The Jin army, now reliant on **private militias and local warlords**, struggled to mount a coherent defense.

What had been regional unrest escalated into full-blown collapse. Entire provinces fell to foreign rule. In 311 CE, the Jin capital **Luoyang was sacked**. In 316 CE, **Chang'an**, the backup capital, fell as well. Northern China was lost.

Collapse of Central Command

With the north in ruins, the Jin court fled south and established a new base in **Jiankang** (modern-day Nanjing). But this was a defensive gesture, not a recovery plan. The empire was split, and the court's authority was no longer respected.

The military response was inconsistent and often **left to regional warlords**, who defended their areas as they saw fit—sometimes cooperating, sometimes fighting each other. With no **unified command** or strategy, the central government functioned in name only.

Even fortresses, once symbols of imperial power, **turned to ruins**—either destroyed by enemies or abandoned due to lack of supplies. The empire's physical infrastructure crumbled alongside its political one.

The Jin Dynasty's downfall wasn't caused by a single enemy—it was the result of a **leadership vacuum**, internal decay, and an empire unable to adapt to new kinds of warfare. What followed was one of the darkest periods in Chinese history: the **Sixteen Kingdoms era**, a time of warlord states, constant invasions, and national fragmentation.

7.2 Southern Survival

Retreat, Rebuild, Resist—How the Eastern Jin Clung to Power South of the Yangtze

The fall of Luoyang and Chang'an marked the end of Jin dominance in northern China. But it did not spell the death of the dynasty itself. Rather than perish completely, the Jin court **fled south**, crossing the Yangtze River and reestablishing their capital in **Jiankang** (modern-day Nanjing). This move transformed Jin into a **regional power**, one defined not by conquest but by survival—shielded by geography, supported by naval innovation, and sustained by a reluctant but resolute military.

Flight to the South

The relocation of the imperial court was not just symbolic—it was strategic. The **Yangtze River** served as a massive natural barrier between the war-torn north and the relatively stable south. The Jin court brought with it **refugees, scholars, and loyal military officers**, many of whom had northern roots and a strong desire to one day reclaim their homeland.

Settling in Jiankang allowed the Jin to consolidate what remained of their power. They rebuilt administrative systems, reestablished contact with southern elites, and began preparing for a long-term defense. Though weakened, they were not finished.

One of their greatest assets became **river-based defenses**. The Yangtze acted as both moat and highway—hard for northern cavalry to cross, yet ideal for moving troops and supplies. The **Jin navy gained strategic dominance** on the river, creating a buffer zone that the northern states struggled to penetrate.

Defensive Adaptations

Survival in the south required a change in military thinking. The Jin army could no longer rely on large standing forces to hold wide-open plains. Instead, they developed **mobile defense units**—smaller, more agile forces stationed at key river crossings, coastal ports, and mountain passes.

City garrisons were reinforced, especially along the Yangtze, with layered walls, elevated signal towers, and stockpiled provisions. These towers allowed the Jin to **relay warnings quickly** across great distances, giving commanders time to position their troops effectively. The entire southern defense grid became a reactive system—flexible, but coordinated.

Just as important was the **use of geography** as a defense mechanism. The south's rivers, swamps, and hills posed challenges to invaders used to the flatlands of the north. Jin commanders learned to **use terrain to slow or trap enemy forces**, ambushing them in ravines or forcing them into narrow passes where superior numbers meant less.

While the court struggled with internal politics, field commanders—many descended from northern aristocracy—focused on maintaining the delicate balance between holding the line and exhausting limited manpower.

Attempts at Reunification

Despite being on the defensive, the Jin did not abandon dreams of a unified China. Several emperors and generals launched **northern expeditions**, attempting to reclaim lost territory from the various nomadic and warlord regimes that had sprung up across the former heartland.

Some of these campaigns had **initial success**, particularly when local populations rose up in support of returning Han rule. However, most efforts eventually **stalled or failed**, due to overextended supply lines, difficult terrain, or betrayal by unreliable allies.

Perhaps most damaging were the **strategic missteps** made by the Jin court itself—dispatching forces too late, undermining promising generals, or shifting priorities mid-campaign. The memory of the north haunted the southern court, but ambition often exceeded capability.

The Eastern Jin never regained full control of China. But through adaptability, naval strength, and defensive cunning, it survived nearly two centuries longer than many expected. Its endurance laid the foundation for future southern dynasties and preserved Chinese culture through one of its darkest eras of division.

7.3 Lessons from Decline

What the Fall of Jin Teaches Us About Military Mismanagement

While the Eastern Jin Dynasty endured longer than many of its peers, its survival was tenuous and reactive. By the time the dynasty finally fell, it was clear that the roots of its decline had been long planted. The fall of Jin offers not just a historical endpoint—but a case study in **how military and political systems fail when they resist adaptation**.

Overreliance on Elites

One of the core weaknesses of the Jin regime was its **dependence on hereditary aristocrats** to lead both civil and military institutions. In times of crisis, loyalty and performance should have outweighed bloodline. But Jin persisted in appointing generals based on **noble rank instead of merit**, leading to widespread inefficiency.

This elite class often favored **civil affairs over military necessity**, prizing Confucian virtue and literary education over martial capability. As a result, many military campaigns were **undermined by court interference** and **ideological rigidity**. Field commanders lacked autonomy. Civilian officials second-guessed experienced generals, and warfare was treated as an unfortunate necessity—rather than a critical aspect of national survival.

Competence went unrewarded, while incompetence was tolerated if politically convenient. This dynamic poisoned morale, stifled initiative, and repelled capable men from serving.

Resistance to Reform

Throughout its rule, the Jin court proved **reluctant to reform** even as the geopolitical environment changed dramatically. The dynasty clung to outdated structures inherited from the Han, failing to modernize its institutions in response to new threats.

This stagnation manifested clearly in the **reuse of obsolete tactics**—especially the overreliance on static infantry formations and fortress defense. While their northern enemies innovated with mobile cavalry and combined arms, Jin forces remained grounded in doctrines suited for a different era.

The court also **refused to invest in new arms or engineering**, instead depending on legacy arsenals and inherited stockpiles. Few advancements were made in siege warfare, mobility, or communication systems. The result was a military increasingly **outclassed by more adaptive enemies**, especially the nomadic and hybrid regimes forming in the north.

Even when confronted with repeated failures, reform efforts were often superficial or **sabotaged by entrenched interests**. Conservatism was mistaken for stability, and innovation was seen as a threat.

Vulnerability to Outsiders

Jin's failure to secure its borders was not a matter of bad luck—it was a product of strategic blindness. The dynasty **ignored or underestimated rising threats along its frontiers**, dismissing nomadic tribes as inferior and incapable of organized conquest. When warning signs emerged—raids, refugee movements, and internal unrest—they were often met with minimal or delayed responses.

The result was a **series of catastrophic incursions** that led to the fall of both capitals in the early 4th century. Even after relocating south, Jin remained vulnerable due to poor resource allocation, overstretched supply lines, and **growing ethnic tensions** within the empire.

Instead of integrating frontier populations, Jin officials often treated them with **distrust or outright hostility**, further alienating potential allies. Efforts to sinicize or co-opt tribal leaders were minimal compared to earlier dynasties like the Han. In this climate of **mutual suspicion**, small problems quickly turned into revolts, defections, or full-scale invasions.

The final blow came not from a single battle, but from decades of **declining discipline**, wasted potential, and a failure to evolve. The Jin Dynasty serves as a warning: **even great states fall when they refuse to learn, adapt, and empower those who can lead in crisis.**

With the fall of Jin, China entered the fractured era of the **Sixteen Kingdoms** and **Northern and Southern Dynasties**—a dark age of endless war, shifting alliances, and cultural upheaval. Yet from this turmoil, new powers would rise—and with them, new ideas in military strategy.

Chapter 8: Sui and Tang—The Return of Imperial Might

8.1 Sui Unification Campaigns

Infrastructure, Speed, and the Cost of Overextension

After centuries of fragmentation, the rise of the **Sui Dynasty** in the late 6th century marked a brief but intense resurgence of imperial ambition. Through rapid military campaigns and large-scale infrastructure projects, the Sui briefly reunified China under a centralized government. Their success, however, was as short-lived as it was impressive—**a victory built on unstable foundations**, where speed and scale replaced sustainability.

Grand Canal and Troop Movement

One of the Sui Dynasty's boldest undertakings was the construction of the **Grand Canal**—a colossal engineering project that connected the Yangtze River in the south with the Yellow River in the north. While originally intended to support trade and tax collection, the canal quickly became a **military superhighway**.

It enabled the **rapid movement of troops and supplies**, cutting weeks off campaign timelines. Armies could be shifted between regions in record time, with ships carrying grain, weapons, and reinforcements directly to the front lines. This kind of **strategic mobility** had never been seen before in Chinese warfare.

However, the canal's construction relied heavily on **forced labor**, with hundreds of thousands conscripted under brutal conditions. While the infrastructure gave the Sui military an edge, it also sowed the seeds of civil unrest. Still, in military terms, the canal was a game-changer—**a logistical artery that made fast war possible**.

Crushing Southern Resistance

With their base in the north, the Sui turned their attention to consolidating control over the south, where former Chen Dynasty loyalists held out. The Sui response was swift and overwhelming.

They deployed **river fleets**, leveraging the Grand Canal and other waterways to strike deep into southern territory. Unlike earlier dynasties that moved cautiously, the Sui favored **blitz-style warfare**—quick, overwhelming assaults that combined **naval power, cavalry, and infantry in coordinated attacks**.

One key innovation was their **combined arms strategy**. Instead of treating army branches separately, the Sui integrated them on the field. Naval squadrons ferried troops to soft targets, cavalry struck retreating forces, and infantry established control. Cities fell rapidly, and resistance was crushed with decisive brutality.

The conquest of the south was effective but left a trail of **resentment and depopulated regions**. The speed of the campaigns outpaced administrative consolidation, and many areas simmered with rebellion even after formal surrender.

Korean Invasion Failure

Flush with victory, the Sui emperor **Yang Guang** (Emperor Yang) turned his attention outward—most notably toward **Goguryeo**, one of the Three Kingdoms of Korea. Believing China had regained its rightful strength, he launched a massive invasion. It would become one of the most disastrous campaigns in imperial history.

The Sui deployed vast naval and land forces, but they were **undermined by harsh climate, poor planning, and thin supply lines**. River routes became choked with wreckage and debris. Monsoons destroyed flotillas. The Korean defenders used **guerrilla tactics, fortified terrain, and ambushes** to maximum effect.

Worse, the long march and failed sieges drained China's treasury and morale. **Tens of thousands of troops died not in battle, but from hunger, illness, and exhaustion**. The campaign, repeated multiple times despite growing opposition, eventually triggered internal revolts.

The empire, built on speed and control, suddenly found itself **unable to maintain order at home**.

The Sui's military legacy is a cautionary tale of extremes. They demonstrated how **logistics and speed could unify a fractured realm**, but also how **overreach and overreliance on brute force could undo an empire just as quickly**. Their rise cleared the path for the **Tang Dynasty**, who would learn from their failures—and elevate Chinese warfare to new heights.

8.2 Tang Military System

Militia, Mobility, and the Machinery of Imperial Control

The Tang Dynasty (618–907 CE) is often remembered for its cultural brilliance, economic prosperity, and expansive diplomacy—but none of this would have been possible without its robust and flexible military system. Evolving from the failures of the Sui, the Tang created a structure that could both defend the realm and expand it. This system—rooted in a blend of **militia-style service, elite specialization, and mobile command**—enabled the Tang to project power across deserts, rivers, mountains, and borders.

Fubing Militia System

At the heart of the early Tang military was the **Fubing system**, a decentralized militia model that drew heavily from the peasantry. **Peasant-soldiers were organized into regional units**, stationed in their hometowns and called up for active duty during specific campaigns or defensive needs.

- These troops served on a **rotational basis**, typically a few months a year, allowing them to maintain their farms while remaining combat-ready.

- This created a model of **military-civilian integration**, where soldiers were not separate from society but part of it, deeply invested in the defense of their communities and empire.

- Units were trained locally and often attached to specific regions, ensuring **loyalty and familiarity with local terrain**.

The Fubing system reduced the need for a large standing army, easing financial burdens while maintaining readiness. However, as the dynasty aged and threats became more complex, the limits of this model would be tested.

Command Hierarchy

To coordinate both militia and regular forces, the Tang relied on a sophisticated **command structure**:

- At the top were **Imperial Guards**, elite troops stationed in the capital, tasked with protecting the emperor and quelling internal dissent.

- In the provinces, authority fell to **regional commanders known as Jiedushi**. Initially designed to provide flexible regional defense, these commanders held both military and civil power—eventually becoming a double-edged sword.

- Within the field armies, **elite cavalry units formed the backbone of mobile operations**. These soldiers were well-trained, heavily armed, and often drawn from aristocratic or tribal backgrounds.

The Tang combined strict hierarchy with regional autonomy, enabling **quick deployment and adaptive defense**. However, as Jiedushi grew too powerful and independent, they would later challenge central authority, contributing to the Tang's decline.

Emphasis on Mobility

More than previous dynasties, the Tang emphasized **speed, maneuverability, and flexibility**. Their forces operated across vast frontiers—from the deserts of Central Asia to the river deltas of the south.

- **Mounted archers**, often recruited from Turkic or steppe peoples, formed the cutting edge of the Tang's mobile forces. These riders could strike fast, harass enemy formations, and retreat before counterattack.

- **Riverine armies**, especially in the Yangtze basin, utilized coordinated fleets to protect trade, suppress rebellions, and launch inland campaigns.

- In open terrain, Tang commanders employed **open field tactics**, favoring flanking maneuvers, cavalry charges, and complex signaling systems over static formations.

The combination of **flexible logistics, cavalry dominance**, and **integrated command** allowed the Tang to dominate East Asia militarily for over a century. They defeated Tibetans, Turks, Koreans, and internal rebels through superior coordination and long-range mobility.

The Tang military system stands as one of ancient China's most effective. It fused **militia discipline, elite specialization, and geographic adaptability**, enabling the dynasty to build one of the largest empires in Chinese history. Yet, as later chapters will reveal, even the strongest systems can falter when regional power begins to rival imperial authority.

8.3 Frontier Expansion

From the Deserts of Central Asia to Internal Collapse

At its height, the Tang Dynasty projected Chinese power farther than any dynasty before it. Tang armies marched across the deserts of Central Asia, tangled with Tibetan warlords in the west, and extended influence deep into Southeast Asia and Korea. But expansion came at a price. Long campaigns strained supply lines, bred overconfidence, and ultimately exposed the limits of imperial control. The Tang's far-flung frontiers brought not only glory—but vulnerability.

Central Asia Campaigns

The Tang saw Central Asia not just as a buffer zone but as a strategic prize. Control over the Silk Road meant access to wealth, alliances, and influence across Eurasia. Tang generals—especially **Gao Xianzhi**, a Korean-born commander—pushed deep into modern-day Uzbekistan, Afghanistan, and Kazakhstan, clashing with local rulers and steppe confederacies.

This culminated in the **Battle of Talas (751 CE)**, where Tang forces met the **Abbasid Caliphate** in what is now Kyrgyzstan. The battle was significant not only for the Tang's defeat—exacerbated by the defection of Turkic mercenaries—but also for the **resulting cultural exchanges**. Chinese papermaking, according to many historians, spread westward as a result of this clash.

Yet Talas revealed a deeper problem: the further the Tang pushed, the more **unsustainable their logistics became**. **Long supply lines** had to cross deserts, mountains, and hostile tribes. Reinforcements were slow. Garrisons became isolated. Campaigns that once brought prestige now bled the empire's strength.

Tibet and the Western Campaigns

To the southwest, the Tang struggled with the powerful **Tibetan Empire**, whose cavalry and mountain tactics challenged even the Tang's seasoned commanders. The Tibetans launched frequent raids, seized key western territories, and briefly occupied the Tang capital **Chang'an** in 763 CE.

The Tang military adapted by deploying **terrain specialists**, establishing **fortified checkpoints** on high-altitude passes, and engaging in **guerrilla warfare** to counter Tibetan mobility. Still, the frontier war remained a **stalemate**—too difficult to win decisively, too important to ignore.

Diplomacy often followed bloodshed. Tang emperors attempted **"diplomacy through force"**, demanding tribute after victories and offering royal marriages after setbacks. These gestures masked a truth: **the Tang were increasingly overextended**, and the cracks were beginning to show.

Internal Rebellions

The empire's outward strength disguised growing internal fragility. The **Fubing system**, once a pillar of Tang power, began to break down. Long campaigns kept troops away from their farms for years, undermining the rotational model. Increasingly, emperors relied on **professional armies under regional generals**—men who began to wield power independent of the court.

The breaking point came in 755 CE, when **General An Lushan**, a trusted frontier commander, rebelled with a massive force. The **An Lushan Rebellion** lasted nearly eight years, killed millions, and devastated the imperial economy. It wasn't just a military revolt—it was a collapse of trust between emperor and general.

After the rebellion, the Fubing system was **formally dismantled**, replaced by mercenary and regional armies. While this stabilized the empire in the short term, it empowered **warlords and provincial governors**, accelerating decentralization. The Tang never fully recovered.

The Tang Dynasty reached farther than any of its predecessors—but its very success sowed the seeds of its decline. The lessons are clear: **ambition without infrastructure is fragility in disguise**, and military power must always be balanced by internal coherence.

Chapter 9: Song Dynasty—Innovation Under Pressure

9.1 Military Challenges

How Internal Restraints and External Threats Shaped a Cautious Empire

The Song Dynasty (960–1279 CE) is widely celebrated for its scientific breakthroughs, economic vitality, and artistic refinement. But beneath this golden surface was a military system burdened by **hesitation, political meddling, and near-constant foreign pressure**. While other dynasties expanded outward, the Song often struggled to defend what it already held. The reason? A military **hamstrung by internal distrust and a leadership structure that prioritized control over command.**

Constant Northern Threats

From its inception, the Song faced serious threats along its northern borders. Unlike earlier dynasties that dealt with fragmented nomadic tribes, the Song contended with **organized, militarized states** such as:

- The **Khitan-led Liao Dynasty**, which controlled large swaths of Manchuria and Northern China.

- The **Jurchen-led Jin Dynasty**, which would eventually capture the Song capital of Kaifeng.

- Later, the **Mongol Empire**, whose conquests would bring the entire dynasty to a catastrophic end.

These adversaries had **well-trained cavalry, better knowledge of frontier terrain, and centralized command structures**—advantages the Song rarely matched. The terrain itself—rugged, mountainous, and difficult to patrol—favored raiders and mobile armies over static defense. Yet Song defenses in the north were often **spread thin**, with key regions **under-garrisoned or reliant on slow reinforcements.**

Civilian Control of the Military

The Song emperors, burned by memories of the An Lushan Rebellion and warlord rule during the Tang's collapse, prioritized **civilian dominance over the military**. Scholar-officials, many of whom passed the civil service exams, were often **placed above or alongside career generals**, stifling battlefield decision-making.

- **Generals lacked autonomy**, often having to consult distant courts before taking action.

- Orders were delayed, and commanders **risked punishment for perceived overreach**, even when acting in defense.

- **Scholar-official dominance** created a command culture where loyalty to the emperor was prized over tactical competence.

This system ensured the emperor's control—but at the cost of battlefield initiative. **Caution replaced creativity**, and **micromanagement slowed response times** to raids and invasions.

Internal Dissent and Structural Paralysis

Compounding the military's external pressures were **internal political divisions**. The imperial court was often split between reformers, conservatives, and opportunists, each with conflicting visions for defense spending, general appointments, and military policy.

- **Overlapping authority** between the Ministry of War, local officials, and the emperor's inner circle led to policy gridlock.

- **Budget constraints** limited investment in frontier infrastructure and troop salaries, even as threats escalated.

- Disagreements over strategy—whether to appease, defend, or preempt enemies—often resulted in **timid, compromised plans that pleased no one**.

These structural flaws turned the Song army into a **reactive force**, reliant on temporary fixes, mercenary help, or tribute payments to buy peace.

The Song Dynasty's military challenges weren't the result of weak soldiers or incapable generals—they were systemic. By design, the dynasty sacrificed **flexibility and initiative** for the sake of **stability and control**. It was a decision that would leave China vulnerable to rising powers and eventually cost the Song their empire.

9.2 Technological Breakthroughs

Gunpowder, Ships, and Strategy in an Age of Defensive Ingenuity

The Song Dynasty may have been militarily cautious, but it was never intellectually stagnant. Faced with aggressive neighbors and political constraints, Song engineers and commanders turned to **technology as their great equalizer**. In this period, Chinese warfare witnessed some of the most pivotal breakthroughs in pre-modern military history—particularly with **gunpowder, naval engineering, and siegecraft**.

Gunpowder Weapons

The Song Dynasty was the first in world history to deploy **gunpowder as a military weapon** on a wide scale. Initially used for shock and confusion, it soon evolved into a deadly arsenal.

- **Fire arrows and bombs**—the earliest battlefield uses—combined gunpowder with archery or thrown projectiles. These devices terrified enemies unfamiliar with loud, fiery weapons.

- **Gunpowder bombs** filled with shrapnel were hurled from trebuchets or slung by hand, used in both open battle and city sieges.

- By the 13th century, **early cannons**—essentially metal or bamboo tubes—began appearing on the battlefield. Though primitive, they were used to break up enemy formations and damage siege equipment.

These weapons played a critical role in **city defense**, giving Song troops an edge when defending walled settlements from numerically superior foes. Explosive deterrents disrupted cavalry charges and siege towers before they reached the walls.

Naval Dominance

While Song armies struggled on land, their navy was **a dominant force**, particularly along the Yangtze River and southern coasts. The dynasty poured resources into building a **formidable fleet**, both for defense and logistics.

- **Paddlewheel ships**, powered by human or animal labor, enabled fast movement along rivers, regardless of wind conditions. These vessels carried troops, supplies, and siege equipment.

- One of the most feared innovations was the **waterborne flamethrower**. These used a double-pump system to spray flammable liquids—likely a mixture of oil and gunpowder—at enemy vessels.

- Larger warships featured **ironclad plating**, making them resistant to arrows and fire. These ships could serve as floating fortresses during river battles or blockades.

The Song navy's engineering allowed it to **control key river crossings, defend trade routes, and outmaneuver northern horse-based armies** that lacked significant naval capabilities.

Siege Engineering

In a time when most battles ended in **city sieges**, the Song invested heavily in defensive and offensive siege technology. Their innovations made them one of the most advanced siege warfare states of the medieval world.

- **Counterweight trebuchets**, imported and adapted from Central Asia, offered increased range and precision compared to traditional traction-powered versions. These could launch heavier projectiles with greater force—ideal for demolishing enemy towers or walls.

- City planners reinforced defenses with **deep moats and tripwire alarm systems**, giving defenders time to organize against infiltrators or scaling ladders.

- To combat the threat of flaming projectiles, engineers developed **flame-resistant barriers**—often using wet hides, mud layers, and stone coatings to protect wooden gates and ramparts.

These innovations reflected a **defensive doctrine based on delay and attrition**, leveraging engineering to sap enemy morale, stall invasions, and buy time for diplomatic or logistical responses.

The Song Dynasty was not defined by conquest—but by its ability to endure. Through **technological innovation**, the Song managed to hold off better-organized foes for centuries. In doing so, it not only preserved the empire's culture and economy but also **pushed military science forward in ways that would ripple across the world**—from the Mongol steppes to the battlefields of Europe.

9.3 Notable Defenses

Holding the Line: Kaifeng, Skirmishes, and the Limits of Technology

Though the Song Dynasty is often seen as militarily conservative, its **defensive campaigns were marked by resilience, clever tactics, and moments of astonishing bravery**. From city sieges to border outposts, Song commanders and soldiers fought hard against superior forces. Yet, the dynasty's most dramatic defenses often revealed a deeper truth—**technology alone couldn't compensate for fragmented leadership and political hesitation**.

Battle of Kaifeng

One of the most iconic events of the Northern Song period was the **siege of Kaifeng** by the Jurchen-led Jin Dynasty in 1126. As the capital city, Kaifeng was a well-fortified urban hub—ringed with walls, guarded by a river network, and equipped with siege defenses. But when Jin forces descended, the Song court found itself **fatally unprepared**.

- Defenders used **traps, fire bombs, and barricades** to repel initial assaults. Oil-filled pits, flaming carts, and collapsing bridges stalled enemy progress in the narrow streets.

- The city became a symbol of **last-stand urban warfare**, with civilian volunteers, scholars, and soldiers fighting together in chaotic melees.

- However, **diplomatic missteps and indecisiveness** at court—combined with delayed reinforcements—undermined the defense. The emperor's reluctance to empower bold generals proved costly.

Ultimately, Kaifeng fell not from a lack of effort, but from a **lack of unified direction**. The city's fall marked the collapse of the Northern Song, pushing the court south and beginning the Southern Song era.

Border Skirmishes and Tactical Defense

While Kaifeng highlighted large-scale failure, many **lesser-known border defenses** revealed the Song army's adaptability on the frontier.

- Along the northwestern plains, Song forces built **fortress lines and outposts**, designed to intercept small raiding parties from the Jin and Mongols. These were often staffed by elite **fast-response units**, trained to move swiftly between strongpoints.

- Commanders frequently used **feigned retreats**, drawing enemies into traps where gunpowder bombs, arrows, and spike pits inflicted heavy casualties.

- Though underfunded and outnumbered, these outposts **delayed enemy momentum**, buying critical time for political or diplomatic maneuvering.

These border fights were rarely decisive, but they showed how **tactical creativity and preparation** could hold off superior cavalry—at least temporarily.

Lessons from Defeat

Despite engineering brilliance and individual heroism, many Song defenses ended in defeat. Why? Because innovation wasn't backed by institutional flexibility or confident leadership.

- There was an **over-dependence on technology**—gunpowder, ships, and walls were used as a crutch, rather than paired with bold strategy or mobile tactics.

- **Morale frequently eroded** due to court indecision, lack of rewards for service, and distrust between civilian and military leaders. Soldiers fought bravely, but many felt abandoned or micromanaged.

- Perhaps most critically, **leadership presence was often absent**. Unlike Tang emperors who occasionally led in person or empowered dynamic generals, the Song court **remained insulated**, issuing decrees from far behind the front lines.

Victory in warfare isn't just about weapons. It's about vision, speed, and unity. The Song's greatest weakness wasn't in its soldiers or its inventions—it was in its inability to **trust commanders, act swiftly, and inspire the front lines**.

The defensive campaigns of the Song Dynasty reflect both ingenuity and tragedy. They teach us that while technology can tip the scales, **wars are still won by cohesive leadership, empowered commanders, and the morale of those who fight**. As the Southern Song would soon learn, even a phoenix must rise while under siege.

Chapter 10: Yuan Dynasty—The Mongol War Machine

10.1 Khan's Invasion

Terror, Tactics, and the Beginning of a New Empire

When the Mongols turned their gaze south toward China, they did not come as mere raiders. They came as an **engineered force of devastation**, blending psychological warfare, superior mobility, and strategic ruthlessness. Unlike their nomadic predecessors, the Mongols—led by **Genghis Khan and his heirs**—didn't simply strike and retreat. They aimed to conquer and integrate. Their invasion didn't just challenge Chinese defenses—it redefined warfare in East Asia.

Psychological Warfare

Before the first arrow flew, the Mongols had already won half the battle—**by spreading fear**.

- They relied heavily on **rumors and terror tactics**, ensuring that news of their massacres traveled faster than their armies. Entire cities surrendered preemptively just to avoid a repeat of what happened in places like Zhongdu (modern-day Beijing).

- **Mass executions** followed resistance. Towns that refused to yield were razed, populations wiped out or enslaved. This was not mindless cruelty—it was **calculated punishment** designed to break the enemy's will.

- Their use of **city-burning tactics** reinforced the message: submission meant survival. Defiance meant total annihilation.

This strategy allowed the Mongols to conquer **dozens of cities without prolonged sieges**, as fear hollowed out resistance from within.

Speed and Maneuver

The heart of the Mongol war machine was its unmatched **mobility**.

- The **horse relay system**—a network of mounted couriers and supply riders—enabled rapid communication across vast distances. Orders from Khan could reach multiple fronts in days, while Chinese commanders still waited for courier pigeons or slow-moving carts.

- Mongol warriors, each traveling with multiple horses, could **ride for days without rest**, repositioning entire units overnight. They struck where defenders least expected.

- Their **compound bows**, made from horn, sinew, and wood, were light, accurate, and deadly—even at full gallop. These weapons out-ranged Chinese crossbows and were effective in both open plains and forested terrain.

The result was a battlefield advantage that left traditional Chinese armies **slow, fragmented, and outmaneuvered**.

Local Adaptation

What truly set the Mongols apart wasn't just destruction—it was **pragmatic assimilation**.

- After encountering heavily fortified cities in northern China, they **recruited Chinese engineers and defected siege specialists**. Rather than rely on brute force alone, they **integrated Song-style siege tactics** into their strategy.

- **Catapults, trebuchets, and gunpowder weapons** were soon turned against Chinese strongholds, combining the Mongols' mobile cavalry with devastating siege firepower.

- They also adjusted their command structure to suit local conditions. Though their hierarchy was fluid and tribal by origin, they empowered **local commanders** when needed and **respected competence over bloodline**—mirroring Legalist military principles once seen in Qin reforms.

The Mongols did not care if a tactic was foreign or unfamiliar. If it worked, they used it. This cultural pragmatism made them **unpredictable and lethal**. They could annihilate one city, then govern the next with tolerance—offering religious freedom, trade incentives, and local autonomy under Mongol rule.

The Mongol invasion under the Yuan banner wasn't just a foreign conquest—it was a military evolution. China's ancient defenses, built over centuries, collapsed in a matter of years. Not because they were weak, but because the Mongols had mastered the ultimate formula: **fear plus speed plus adaptability**.

10.2 Kublai Khan's Empire

From Nomadic Conquest to Imperial Administration

By the time **Kublai Khan** declared the founding of the **Yuan Dynasty** in 1271, the Mongols were no longer just desert raiders. They were emperors. And Kublai, unlike his grandfather Genghis Khan, sought more than conquest—he wanted to rule China not as a foreign occupier, but as a legitimate Son of Heaven. To do that, he had to fuse **Mongol military dominance with Chinese administrative sophistication**. It was a monumental task—and an uneasy balance.

Sinicization of the Military

Kublai understood that raw force alone couldn't govern an empire as vast and complex as China. He moved swiftly to **integrate Mongol and Chinese systems**, both militarily and bureaucratically.

- One major shift was the **use of Chinese bureaucrats** in provincial and military administration. While key positions remained in Mongol hands, Chinese advisors and generals were vital to maintaining supply lines, local recruitment, and tax collection.

- Kublai established a **standing army system**, including Mongols, Chinese, and subject peoples (like Central Asians and Persians), organized in a tiered ethnic structure. Mongols formed elite units, while Chinese and others filled support roles.

- This structure ensured loyalty at the top but limited career advancement for Chinese commanders—a choice that **stirred resentment and limited innovation** within the ranks.

Kublai's military was no longer just a cavalry swarm—it was a **hybrid machine**, wielding siege weapons, naval fleets, and garrison networks.

Naval Ambitions and Failed Invasions

Kublai's vision went beyond continental dominance. He dreamed of a pan-Asian empire, stretching across oceans and jungles. This ambition led to some of the most **costly military failures in Chinese history**.

- He invested heavily in **naval fleet development**, commissioning large ships, floating docks, and specialized marine divisions. These efforts allowed for the conquest of the Southern Song in 1279—a victory achieved by **blockading river cities and cutting off supply chains**.

- Emboldened, Kublai ordered invasions of **Japan** in 1274 and again in 1281. While the Yuan fleets initially made landfall, they were ultimately destroyed by typhoons—**the famed "kamikaze" or divine winds**. These disasters sank thousands of ships and killed tens of thousands of troops.

- In **Vietnam**, the Mongols faced a different problem: guerrilla resistance and harsh jungle terrain. Despite early success, they couldn't hold ground. Disease, ambushes, and logistical nightmares **turned victory into retreat**.

These defeats revealed a hard limit: **the Mongol war machine was built for open steppe and plains**, not tropical jungles or typhoon-prone coastlines.

Control Through Fear and Infrastructure

While military campaigns faltered abroad, Kublai tightened control at home through a blend of **fear and logistical mastery**.

- He implemented a vast **taxation network**, funding both his military and the opulent court in Dadu (modern-day Beijing).

- **Post stations (Yam)**—adapted from the old Mongol horse relay system—became nodes for communication, intelligence, and supply transfers. These allowed for **fast deployment of troops and orders across the empire**.

- Major cities were turned into **garrison strongholds**, with Mongol or loyal troops stationed to enforce order, deter rebellion, and oversee regional administration.

The Yuan state relied on **command and infrastructure rather than consent**. Stability was enforced, not earned. Though trade thrived along the Silk Road and through maritime routes, discontent simmered in the countryside.

Kublai Khan's empire was a bold experiment in blending nomadic ferocity with imperial sophistication. But in chasing empire-wide control and external conquest, **he stretched the limits of Mongol dominance—and began the long unraveling of Yuan authority**.

10.3 Mongol Military Legacy

Fusion, Overreach, and the Lessons of Collapse

The Mongols didn't just conquer China—they transformed its military landscape. Under the Yuan Dynasty, China experienced an era where **steppe mobility fused with imperial bureaucracy**, and warfare became more global, adaptive, and brutal. But the very tools that enabled Mongol success—speed, fear, and force—also revealed deep weaknesses when faced with internal resistance and strategic overstretch. Their legacy is one of both **military brilliance and fatal inflexibility**.

Blended Tactics and Hybrid Army Culture

The Mongols introduced a form of warfare that **China had never seen before**—highly mobile, multiethnic, and devastatingly effective.

- The Yuan military was a **hybrid machine**, blending **steppe cavalry tactics** with **Chinese siege warfare and engineering**. Catapults, sappers, and flame weapons were paired with fast, coordinated cavalry maneuvers.

- This **hybridized army culture** incorporated not just Chinese troops, but also Central Asians, Persians, and even Europeans. These multicultural forces brought a **range of techniques**, from crossbow formations to cannon-making.

- The result was **greater battlefield flexibility**. Yuan armies could besiege fortified cities with advanced machinery one day and chase down rebels across mountains the next.

Yet this strength came at a cost: **unity of purpose was fragile**, and loyalty often came from fear or payment—not shared values.

Strategic Weaknesses and Military Overreach

Despite their military power, the Yuan Dynasty suffered from fundamental flaws that **no amount of force could cover**.

- **Strategic overreach** plagued Kublai Khan and his successors. From Japan to Vietnam to Burma, Yuan emperors pursued imperial ambitions **beyond the logistical limits** of their supply chains and naval capabilities.

- The Mongols' core advantage—**brutality as deterrence**—began to backfire. Over time, conquered populations became **resistant to fear**, especially as Yuan rule grew more corrupt and exploitative.

- Perhaps most fatally, the Mongols never fully developed a **comprehensive naval doctrine**. While they could build ships and hire coastal forces, they **lacked the maritime intuition** of their Southern Song predecessors. Sea-based invasions failed repeatedly.

As the Yuan empire expanded geographically, its **capacity to govern and defend it shrank politically**.

The End of Mongol Supremacy

By the 14th century, the empire began to unravel—not from a single defeat, but from **a thousand fractures**.

- **Peasant revolts** erupted across China, most famously the **Red Turban Rebellion**, fueled by famine, tax burdens, and anti-Mongol resentment.

- The **Yuan court grew corrupt and detached**, plagued by factionalism and unable to respond swiftly to crises. Mongol nobles feuded, Chinese officials were mistrusted, and local administrators grew increasingly autonomous.

- These weaknesses created a perfect opening for a new force: the **Ming resistance**, led by Zhu Yuanzhang, a former monk-turned-general. His forces emphasized **grassroots recruitment, clear purpose, and disciplined logistics**—everything the Yuan had lost.

In 1368, the Mongols were driven from Beijing. Their empire in China was finished.

The Mongol military left a paradoxical legacy. It elevated warfare to new levels of speed, scale, and integration—but failed to build the moral and institutional backbone needed to sustain rule. The Yuan era shows us that **force can win empires, but cannot hold them alone**. Discipline, legitimacy, and adaptability are what truly endure.

Chapter 11: Ming Dynasty — Rebuilding from the Ashes

11.1 Restoring the Military System

Zhu Yuanzhang's Blueprint for a Safer Empire

When Zhu Yuanzhang rose from peasant rebel to founding emperor of the **Ming Dynasty**, he did so with a mission: never again would China fall to foreign invaders. The scars of Mongol domination ran deep, and Zhu—who became **Emperor Hongwu**—believed military reform was central to national revival. His military system wasn't just about defense; it was about **restoring Han Chinese pride, imposing centralized order, and erasing the legacy of Yuan misrule**.

Zhu Yuanzhang's Reforms

Zhu took direct control of rebuilding China's armed forces. His reforms were aimed at preventing both **foreign invasion and internal rebellion**.

- He established the **Weisuo system**, a military household registration structure. Families were assigned to hereditary military service, responsible for producing soldiers generation after generation. This gave the state a **standing army without constant recruitment**.

- In return, these households were often granted **land-for-service**, integrating military life with agriculture. Soldiers farmed during peace and fought during war. It was a throwback to earlier militia models, reimagined for long-term stability.

- Command was carefully **reorganized into a strict hierarchy**. Units were ranked by size—guards, battalions, companies—and directly tied to regional administrations.

This system created **military permanence**, rooted in Chinese soil. It was not a hired force. It was a national body, raised to endure.

Revival of Native Pride

The Ming army became a **symbol of Han resurgence**. After a century under Mongol rule, the Hongwu Emperor wanted to build more than muscle—he wanted to cultivate **a Chinese identity tied to military strength**.

- Anti-Mongol sentiment shaped everything from **uniform design to military rituals**. Emblems, banners, and ceremonies reflected **Confucian and imperial symbols** meant to reinforce cultural unity.

- Border defenses were expanded and rebuilt, especially in the north. A **new phase of Great Wall construction** began—focused not on mobility, but **on permanent fortification against nomadic incursions**.

- Foreign customs, religions, and dress were increasingly **banned from military life**, seen as remnants of Yuan decay.

This revivalist approach helped foster morale and unity—but it also led to **insularity**, making Ming forces less adaptive to foreign tactics or innovations.

Problems with Central Control

While Zhu's reforms aimed to stabilize the state, they also revealed deep fears—particularly his **distrust of generals**.

- Independent military power was seen as a threat to imperial authority. As a result, top commanders were often **rotated, purged, or executed** at the emperor's whim.

- **Eunuchs**—traditionally court servants—were increasingly assigned to oversee military affairs. Lacking battlefield experience, they acted as **imperial watchdogs**, undermining professional officers and creating dual lines of command.

- Over time, the system became **overdependent on the emperor's personal oversight**. This worked under Zhu, who was active and forceful, but later emperors lacked his energy or insight—leading to **bureaucratic stagnation and military decline**.

The result was a military that could be massive on paper but sluggish in practice—**rigidly structured, but slow to innovate or respond to crises**.

The Ming Dynasty began with a bold, structured military vision: permanent defense, native pride, and total imperial control. It succeeded in stabilizing China for decades. But the seeds of **over-centralization and paranoia** were already planted—seeds that would sprout into crisis when real enemies tested the empire's strength.

11.2 Defensive Fortifications

Walls, Watchtowers, and the Geography of Security

While many dynasties sought glory through conquest, the Ming Dynasty sought **security through permanence**. Having emerged from the ashes of foreign occupation, Ming rulers poured immense resources into building physical barriers—not just symbolic, but militarily functional. **The fortified empire they built reflected both confidence and fear**: a determination to prevent another Yuan-style invasion, and a deep suspicion of external threats from land and sea.

Great Wall Reconstruction

The most iconic project of Ming fortification was the **rebuilding of the Great Wall**—not as a loose chain of earthworks, but as a **massive, coordinated military structure**.

- **Brick and stone reinforcements** replaced older rammed-earth sections. These durable walls stretched thousands of kilometers, engineered to withstand cavalry charges, siege weapons, and the elements.

- **Beacon towers and signal relays** were spaced along the wall, enabling messages to travel hundreds of kilometers in a single day using smoke by day and fire by night.

- The wall incorporated **anti-cavalry defenses**, including elevated firing platforms, angled bastions, and kill zones where attackers could be funneled into arrow crossfire.

The Ming Great Wall wasn't just symbolic—it was **a logistical and communication network**, manned year-round by garrison troops and equipped to resist mobile northern threats like the Mongols and later the Manchu.

Coastal Defense Systems

While the north demanded walls, the coast required fleets and fortresses. As maritime trade increased, so did the threat of piracy—especially from the **Wokou (Japanese and Chinese pirates)**.

- The Ming constructed **coastal fortifications**—stone towers, garrisoned watchposts, and cannon emplacements—along key stretches of the eastern and southeastern seaboard.

- These defenses included **early gun batteries**, using muzzle-loading cannons and firelances to repel pirate ships and intruders.

- Naval bases were fortified with **drydocks, supply depots, and barracks**, enabling faster deployment of coastal patrols and better coordination during pirate raids.

Though piracy remained a persistent issue, these efforts **reduced large-scale coastal raiding** and protected maritime trade routes that were vital to China's economy.

City Planning for War

Defense wasn't limited to borders—it was baked into the very **layout of Ming cities**.

- Major cities were encircled with **thick walls, deep moats, and outer fields designed as kill zones**—open areas where attackers could be targeted before reaching the walls.

- **Barracks were placed near city centers**, allowing for quick troop deployment to outer gates or key infrastructure in case of an internal uprising or siege.

- Civilian populations were required to participate in **defense drills and preparedness routines**, creating a culture where **war-readiness was a part of urban life**.

Many cities also featured **layered gates and inner citadels**, where leadership could retreat and mount resistance if outer walls were breached.

The Ming approach to defense was holistic. Fortification wasn't an afterthought—it was **a central strategy**, rooted in geography, engineering, and social structure. The result was one of the most heavily fortified states in world history.

But it came at a cost. The focus on defense made the Ming army **reactive rather than innovative**, and heavy investment in walls couldn't always stop political decay from within.

11.3 Major Campaigns

From Mongol Clashes to Korean Alliances—and a Slow, Costly Decline

While the Ming Dynasty is remembered for its fortresses and walls, it was far from passive. In its first two centuries, the Ming engaged in **bold campaigns against northern nomads and foreign invaders**, projecting power across the steppes and seas. Yet by its final century, a pattern of stagnation had taken hold—**costly wars, stretched supply lines, and outdated doctrine**, all fueling the dynasty's decline. Its history of military campaigns reveals **both tactical strength and strategic erosion**.

Ming–Mongol Conflicts

The Ming's first and most persistent threat was the Mongol remnant states to the north. Though the Yuan Dynasty had been expelled from China, its successors—the Northern Yuan—continued to harass Ming borders.

- Early in the dynasty, the Ming won **several decisive cavalry battles**, using disciplined forces and fortified outposts to repel Mongol raids. General Xu Da's early expeditions even pushed deep into Mongol territory.

- After the humiliating **Tumu Crisis in 1449**, where Emperor Zhengtong was captured by the Oirat Mongols, the Ming shifted to **defensive strategies**. The emperor's capture exposed the vulnerability of personal leadership on campaigns.

- In response, the Ming strengthened **frontier forts**, reinforced the Great Wall, and adopted a more **reactive stance**. Mongol incursions continued, but the Ming rarely initiated major counter-invasions thereafter.

These wars kept the Ming army alert but drained resources, pushing the empire toward **military conservatism and static defense**.

The Imjin War (Korea)

The **Imjin War (1592–1598)** marked one of the Ming's most important and complex campaigns—its military support for Korea against Japanese invasion.

- When Japan's Toyotomi Hideyoshi launched an invasion of Korea, the Ming responded with **joint operations alongside Korean forces**, seeing the threat as a direct challenge to regional order.

- The Ming deployed tens of thousands of troops, coordinating with **Korean General Yi Sun-sin**, whose innovative naval tactics—including armored turtle ships—crippled Japanese supply lines.

- This war offered vital **lessons in logistics and naval warfare**. The Ming's slow supply chains and bureaucratic delays exposed weaknesses in command structure, while Korea's agile navy demonstrated the importance of flexibility at sea.

Though the Japanese were eventually driven out, the campaign cost the Ming heavily in manpower, money, and morale—**without clear territorial gains**.

Fall of the Dynasty

By the 17th century, the Ming was besieged not by foreign enemies alone, but by **internal decay and rebellion**.

- Constant warfare, famine, and tax burdens led to widespread **rebellion fatigue**. Peasant uprisings gained momentum, especially under leaders like **Li Zicheng**, who would eventually take Beijing.

- The military suffered from **chronic underfunding**. Commanders couldn't pay troops, maintain supply lines, or upgrade equipment. Desertion and corruption became rampant.

- Despite clear warning signs, the Ming court **failed to reform outdated systems**. The hereditary military household system (Weisuo) had collapsed, generals had limited autonomy, and technological innovation had stalled.

When the **Manchu-led Qing forces crossed the Great Wall**, they didn't conquer a strong empire—they inherited one that had **rotted from within**.

The Ming Dynasty fought hard—but **defensive brilliance couldn't overcome strategic inertia**. From early victories on the steppes to coordinated naval campaigns in Korea, the Ming proved capable. Yet in the end, it was a failure to evolve, to fund, and to empower that doomed their empire to collapse.

Chapter 12: Qing Dynasty — The Last Imperial Army

12.1 Manchu Military Origins

Banners, Brotherhood, and the Conquest of China

The Qing Dynasty, China's last imperial regime, rose not from within the empire, but from beyond its borders. The founders—the **Manchus**—were a semi-nomadic people from the northeast who transformed themselves from tribal warriors into a disciplined, multiethnic force that conquered and ruled the largest territory in Chinese history. Their military success was built on a distinct system of organization and loyalty known as the **Eight Banners**, a model that emphasized **unity, adaptability, and ruthless efficiency.**

Banner System Organization

At the heart of the Qing military lay the **Eight Banners system**, a framework that was more than just military—it was social, political, and cultural.

- Each **Banner** was a unit of administration and command, identified by colored flags (Plain Yellow, Bordered Yellow, Plain White, etc.). These banners divided troops by ethnicity and function while promoting **loyalty through identity.**

- Initially composed entirely of Manchu clans, the structure expanded to include **Mongol and Han Chinese banners**—with leadership and pay still reflecting ethnic hierarchy. This **separation in command** helped prevent mutiny and encouraged cohesion within each group.

- Banner membership was hereditary and communal. Soldiers and their families lived together, trained together, and fought together, reinforcing **family-based loyalty** that bound individuals not just to the state, but to the banner as a tribe.

This system was highly centralized and easy to mobilize—**perfect for rapid expansion and loyalty enforcement** during conquest.

Conquest of China

The Manchu conquest of the Ming was not achieved through numbers alone—it was achieved through **gunpowder, patience, and superior mobility**.

- While known for their cavalry, the Manchus quickly adopted **gunpowder weapons** captured from or copied after Ming arsenals. Matchlock firearms, cannons, and explosive shells were used in sieges and open field combat.

- Their conquest strategy combined **siege tactics, military engineering, and bribery**. Instead of fighting every city, they often encouraged surrender through psychological pressure, diplomacy, and promises of limited looting.

- On the northern frontier, the Manchus maintained a clear **edge in cavalry warfare**. Their horse archers, trained from childhood, could outmaneuver most Ming forces still tied to outdated drill formations and defensive strongholds.

After breaching the Great Wall (with the help of a defected Ming general), the Manchus rolled through a fragmented empire, claiming Beijing and eventually unifying China under the Qing name.

Assimilation and Discipline

Unlike previous conquerors, the Qing rulers knew that **military strength alone wouldn't sustain power**. They moved swiftly to consolidate control through assimilation, discipline, and strategic flexibility.

- Banner troops were trained not only in Manchu techniques but also in **Chinese military doctrine and weaponry**. Firearms units became common, especially in southern campaigns.

- Commands were often issued in **both Manchu and Chinese**, reflecting the Qing commitment to ruling a multiethnic empire without losing their own identity.

- The Qing emphasized **discipline and unity** above all. Desertion was punished severely, officers were rotated to avoid local corruption, and military merit was rewarded—regardless of ethnicity within the banner system.

This created a hybrid military capable of fighting steppe rebels, southern rebels, and Western gunboats alike—at least for a time.

The Manchu military system was built on **structure, loyalty, and smart adaptation**. It didn't just conquer an empire—it held it for centuries. But like all systems, its strength contained the seeds of future weakness: **rigidity, ethnic stratification, and eventual bureaucratic decay**. Still, at its height, the Qing Banner Army was one of the most effective military organizations of the early modern world.

12.2 Stability through Control

Suppressing Dissent, Expanding Borders, and Managing the Empire

Unlike their predecessors, the Qing rulers did not rely on military brilliance alone to govern China—they depended on a strategy of **systemic control**. That meant quelling rebellion before it could grow, integrating loyal non-Manchu forces into their system, and stationing troops across the empire's far reaches. What emerged was a model of **military-backed authoritarian governance**, enforced not just with weapons, but with fear, surveillance, and strategic co-option.

Suppressing Internal Rebellions

The Qing faced major internal challenges throughout their reign, the most notable being the **White Lotus Rebellion** (1794–1804), a millenarian uprising that exposed vulnerabilities in the empire's core.

- In response, the court intensified the use of **brutal legal punishments**. Executions, public torture, and the collective punishment of families sent a message: resistance would not be tolerated.

- This was paired with a psychological strategy often called **"soft terror"**—creating an atmosphere of dread through informant networks, public surveillance, and harsh penalties for dissent, even in speech or rumor.

- Rather than relying solely on Banner troops, the Qing expanded the use of **Han Chinese soldiers** in internal security roles. This allowed the court to suppress fellow Han rebels using **familiar language and tactics**, reducing resistance and suspicion.

It was a mix of force and cultural optics: letting Han crush Han, under Manchu direction.

Dual Military System: Banners and Green Standards

To maintain control, the Qing split their military power between the **Manchu-dominated Banner system** and the more locally integrated **Green Standard Army**.

- The **Green Standard Army**—made up mostly of Han Chinese—handled routine policing, border patrols, and suppression of banditry and rebellion. Unlike Banner troops, they were often stationed long-term in provinces and cities.

- They functioned as a mix of **military and civilian police**, enforcing Qing law, collecting intelligence, and reinforcing imperial authority at the local level.

- The Banner forces, by contrast, remained **elite and mobile**, deployed during major campaigns or emergencies. Coordinated action between the two systems created a balance of **routine control and overwhelming response power**.

This dual structure allowed the Qing to cover a vast territory while limiting the political independence of either force.

Border Expansion and Ethnic Control

Military expansion wasn't just about conquest—it was about locking down territory and suppressing diversity that might challenge the Qing's authority.

- The Qing undertook aggressive campaigns into **Tibet, Xinjiang, and Taiwan**, framing them as efforts to stabilize borders. These campaigns often involved **sieges, mass deportations, and targeted violence**.

- After conquest, the empire established **garrisons and military colonies**—permanent stations of Banner and Green Standard troops tasked with maintaining order and projecting imperial presence.

- In some cases, the Qing pursued **forced migration policies**, moving loyal populations into frontier regions to dilute resistance. Local cultures were repressed, religious practices restricted, and resistance punished by exile or execution.

This method of control was not subtle—but it was effective for decades. By the 18th century, the Qing ruled over **one of the largest and most ethnically diverse empires in the world**, with a military force more focused on **containment than conquest**.

The Qing dynasty mastered control through presence. Troops were everywhere—on city walls, in mountain passes, on riverbanks, and in rural garrisons. Rebellion was never impossible, but it was always dangerous. Yet the very strength of this system—its rigidity, surveillance, and overreliance on fear—would ultimately make it **brittle in the face of modern threats**.

12.3 Resistance to Change

How Stagnation and Conservatism Doomed the Qing War Machine

By the 19th century, the Qing army was no longer the cutting-edge, hybrid force that had conquered China. It had become a **rigid, underfunded institution** clinging to outdated practices in a rapidly changing world. As Western powers brought steamships, rifles, and railroads to Asia, Qing leaders—rooted in Confucian conservatism and fearful of internal chaos—chose hesitation over innovation. That choice would prove fatal.

Avoiding Western Modernization

The Qing court's deep distrust of foreigners translated into a persistent rejection of their military innovations—often to catastrophic effect.

- The empire made **little investment in naval power**, even after seeing Western ironclads dominate in nearby seas. Coastal defenses remained underfunded and fragmented.

- Foreign weapons, like **repeating rifles and breech-loading artillery**, were viewed as unnecessary or incompatible with Chinese tradition. Qing generals often clung to swords, spears, and outdated matchlocks.

- This was not just a technological issue—it was **cultural conservatism**. Many elites believed Chinese civilization was superior and that borrowing from the West risked moral and political decay.

As Western armies stormed Chinese ports with disciplined ranks and modern arms, Qing forces were **still using tactics from centuries prior**.

Failures in Modernization

Some Qing officials saw the writing on the wall and pushed for reform, leading to the **Self-Strengthening Movement (1861–1895)**. But good ideas died in the swamp of corruption, infighting, and delay.

- The movement aimed to modernize arsenals, build shipyards, and send students abroad—but reforms were **poorly coordinated**, and often blocked by conservative factions in court.

- Funds meant for railroads and telegraphs were siphoned off by bureaucrats. Where railways did emerge, they were limited in reach and often sabotaged by those who feared "dragon lines" would anger the spirits of the land.

- Military schools were opened, but instructors lacked combat experience, and the curriculum was fragmented. Meanwhile, Western-trained soldiers returned to find **an army that rejected their expertise**.

Ultimately, China had the form of modernization—but not the function. Reform came **too little, too late**, and with too many internal enemies.

Military Collapse

This stagnation was exposed in a series of devastating defeats that shattered Qing military credibility.

- During the **First and Second Opium Wars** (1839–42, 1856–60), British and French forces easily overran Chinese defenses. Qing troops were **outgunned, outmaneuvered, and outled**.

- The **Taiping Rebellion** (1850–64), one of the deadliest civil wars in history, further drained imperial strength. The Qing had to rely on **regional warlords and private militias** to survive, undermining central authority.

- Finally, the **Boxer Uprising** (1899–1901) revealed how disconnected the Qing had become. Supported by conservative officials, the anti-foreign Boxers attacked missionaries and foreign legations. Western powers retaliated with overwhelming force, occupying Beijing and forcing massive indemnities on the empire.

Each conflict eroded both the military and the myth of imperial power. The Qing army had become a **shell of its former self**, held together by inertia and fear.

In the end, it wasn't foreign invasion or rebellion alone that brought down the Qing—it was **the refusal to adapt**. While other nations embraced the industrial age, Qing leaders clung to outdated hierarchies and illusions of superiority. When change finally came, it came from outside—and the imperial army, once the guardian of the dynasty, **collapsed under the weight of its own stagnation**.

Chapter 13: Weapons, Tools, and Technologies

13.1 Infantry and Cavalry Weapons

Steel, String, and Strategy: The Tools of Ancient Chinese Warfighters

Across thousands of years of Chinese history, the weapons wielded by infantry and cavalry reflected far more than metallurgy—they expressed **strategic values, technological innovation, and cultural ideals**. Chinese armies were not just armed with blades and bows, but with doctrine: combining **discipline, formation tactics, and engineering knowledge** to make every weapon a part of a larger battlefield system.

Swords and Halberds

Blades and polearms were the backbone of close-quarters combat, evolving through dynasties in form and function.

- The **jian**, a straight double-edged sword, was often seen as a gentleman's weapon, favored by officers and elites. More symbolic than practical by the later dynasties, it emphasized **precision and agility**.

- The **dao**, a single-edged curved saber, became the most widely used battlefield sword. Its slashing motion was ideal for cavalry and shock troops, offering greater cutting power and **ease of use for conscripted infantry**.

- The **ji**, a hybrid between spear and dagger-axe, was a versatile polearm used especially in the Zhou and Han periods. With a stabbing point and side blade, it allowed **hooking, slashing, and thrusting** in tight phalanx formations.

Over time, **metallurgy improved blade strength**, with bronze giving way to steel and iron. Weapons became lighter, sharper, and more standardized under state-run armories.

Bows and Crossbows

While melee weapons handled the chaos of close-range combat, the Chinese battlefield was often **decided at a distance**—by volleys of arrows launched with terrifying coordination.

- Traditional bows remained in use across dynasties, with specialized **archer units trained from youth**. Recurve designs provided compact power, especially useful for mounted archers.

- The **crossbow**, however, was the game-changer. Introduced during the Warring States period, it allowed soldiers to fire bolts with lethal force and little training. By the Han Dynasty, crossbows were mass-produced with **interchangeable parts and locking mechanisms**, a marvel of ancient engineering.

- **Repeating crossbows**, such as the Zhuge Nu, offered rapid fire through a magazine-fed design. Though less powerful than single-shot versions, they were useful for **defensive lines and close-range suppression**.

Mounted archery remained a core cavalry tactic, especially in the north, where steppe warfare demanded **speed, range, and accuracy while on horseback**.

Armor and Shields

Defense was as critical as offense—and ancient Chinese armies developed a wide variety of **armor types** suited for geography, role, and dynasty.

- **Leather armor**, hardened with lacquer, was common in early periods due to cost and flexibility. **Bronze and iron scale armor** later provided heavier protection, especially for elite troops.

- **Lamellar armor**—constructed from overlapping plates laced together—offered a balance of mobility and defense, allowing soldiers to move freely while resisting slashes and light projectiles.

- **Shields** ranged from small round versions for mobile infantry to large rectangular wall shields used in defensive formations. They were made from wood, covered in hide, and sometimes reinforced with metal rims.

Each dynasty balanced **armor weight with maneuverability**. Infantry units often wore lighter gear to maintain formation speed, while heavy cavalry—especially under the Tang and Yuan—were outfitted like medieval tanks.

Chinese warfare was never defined by a single weapon—it was defined by **systems thinking**. A sword was only as effective as the formation wielding it. A crossbow only as valuable as the logistics keeping it loaded. Across every dynasty, infantry and cavalry evolved not just in strength, but in **coherence with the military philosophy of their time**.

13.2 Siege and Fortification Tech

Walls, War Machines, and the Science of Taking Cities

While open-field battles decided momentum, it was **siege warfare** that often determined the fate of dynasties. Across ancient and imperial China, the struggle between invaders and defenders became a technological arms race. From towering battering rams to flame-filled ditches, every campaign forced innovation. The art of siege wasn't just about destruction—it was about patience, pressure, and precision.

Siege Engines

Attacking a walled city required more than bravery—it required engineering. Chinese armies deployed an evolving arsenal of **siege machines**, often adapted from or improved upon foreign designs.

- **Battering rams**, mounted on wheels and covered with protective roofing, were used to break down wooden gates or weak stone points. Their rhythmic assault was both physical and psychological.

- **Siege towers**, built as mobile platforms, allowed attackers to scale high walls while protected from archers. Some had pivoting bridges for direct boarding over parapets.

- **Trebuchets**, particularly counterweight versions developed by the Song Dynasty, hurled massive stones, firepots, or even diseased corpses into enemy cities. Their range and destructive power made them the **long-range artillery of their era**.

- **Scaling ladders**, though rudimentary, remained a staple—used in surprise assaults or simultaneous with other distractions.

Chinese sieges were rarely brute-force affairs. They were **timed, planned, and engineered**.

Wall Design and Layered Defenses

To resist these machines, cities responded with layered defenses—**more than just tall walls**.

- City walls evolved from packed-earth to **brick-faced and stone-lined structures**, which resisted siege rams and erosion alike.

- **Layered defense zones** became standard: outer moats, secondary inner walls, watchtowers at intervals, and **gatehouses with murder holes** to trap and ambush attackers.

- Some cities built **angled walls** and curved bastions to better deflect projectiles and eliminate blind spots.

These designs emphasized **delay and attrition**—forcing enemies into bottlenecks where defenders could concentrate force.

- **Moats and traps** added further protection. Moats made undermining or ramming walls difficult, while hidden pits, caltrops, or flame trenches caught advancing troops off guard.

- Ming cities even used **brick layering innovations**, alternating different materials to absorb shock from cannon fire—a rare but forward-thinking method in the pre-modern world.

Defensive Countermeasures

Defenders weren't passive. Siege defense was an art of its own, filled with tactics to **disrupt, delay, or destroy** siege operations.

- **Hot oil and molten metal** were poured from walls onto ladders and siege towers. While sometimes exaggerated in later retellings, boiling water, lime, and tar were effective deterrents.

- **Smoke bombs and fire arrows** disrupted formations and burned wooden siege equipment. Chinese defenders often prepared flammable oil-soaked bundles and coordinated timed ignitions.

- **Underground tunnels** were dug to either collapse enemy trenches or infiltrate siege camps at night. Conversely, defenders used **listening tunnels** to detect enemy sappers and launch surprise counter-digs.

- **Fire breaks and ditches** were built around wooden structures and wall bases, ensuring that attackers couldn't set city walls ablaze or get close with combustible materials.

The longer the siege, the more likely reinforcements or disease would turn the tide. Thus, both sides fought against **not just each other—but time**.

Siege warfare in China blended engineering, patience, and brutality. A wall was never just a wall—it was a symbol, a trap, a battlefield in itself. And every siege was a test: of endurance, of innovation, and of the empire's will to hold its ground.

13.3 Gunpowder and Naval Warfare

Explosive Power and Command of the Waters

China was the birthplace of **gunpowder**—a discovery that would eventually change the world. But long before European cannons battered medieval castles, Chinese armies and navies were already deploying fire-based weapons to **shock, burn, and terrorize** their enemies. From handheld fire lances to ironclad paddlewheel ships, the Chinese integrated explosive power with strategy—though they would later fall behind in global arms races.

Fire Lances, Bombs, and Early Cannons

The earliest gunpowder weapons weren't cannons—they were **extensions of melee combat**, designed for fear as much as destruction.

- **Fire lances** were spear-like weapons with tubes of gunpowder attached to the shaft. Upon ignition, they discharged flame, shrapnel, or projectiles at close range. Initially used to surprise cavalry charges, they were **psychological weapons** as much as functional ones.

- **Gunpowder bombs**, made of bamboo or ceramic shells filled with black powder, were hurled by hand, sling, or trebuchet. They produced loud bangs, flashes, and smoke to **cause chaos in enemy ranks**.

- **Portable cannons** began to appear during the Song Dynasty, often cast in bronze. These early firearms were heavy, slow to reload, and wildly inaccurate—but devastating when properly deployed.

By the Yuan and Ming dynasties, gunpowder was no longer experimental—it was **a battlefield necessity**.

Cannons, Rockets, and Land-Based Artillery

With each dynasty, gunpowder usage became more systematized, especially in siege and defensive warfare.

- **Cannons** evolved from crude tubes to large cast-metal weapons mounted on wheeled carts or fortress walls. In the Ming period, they were used to defend cities and bombard siege formations from distance.

- **Rocket carts**, loaded with dozens of arrow-like missiles propelled by powder tubes, provided a terrifying spectacle—though they were more effective in **psychological warfare** than tactical precision.

- While China pioneered the **use of gunpowder**, later centuries saw the Qing fall behind as European artillery improved. The hesitation to mass-produce advanced firearms would prove a strategic liability by the 19th century.

Still, early Chinese armies had laid the foundation for modern explosives long before others had even discovered the formula.

Naval Advancements and Ship-Based Warfare

China's vast river networks and coastlines demanded naval superiority—especially during the Southern Song and Ming dynasties.

- **Paddlewheel ships**, powered by teams of rowers, allowed for enhanced maneuverability and speed. These ships could navigate tight rivers and turn sharply—crucial in close naval engagements.

- The Ming era introduced **flamethrowers mounted on ships**, using bellows and burning oil to devastate enemy fleets. Some vessels carried **catapults and bombs** on their decks, turning ships into mobile artillery platforms.

- There are even historical records of **iron-plated ships**, or proto-ironclads, built with reinforced hulls to resist fire and ramming. While not as advanced as later Western ironclads, they were an early experiment in **defensive naval design**.

The peak of Chinese naval power came under Admiral Zheng He, whose 15th-century treasure fleets dwarfed anything in Europe—but these expeditions were quickly halted by imperial order, marking a **sharp retreat from maritime dominance**.

Gunpowder was China's gift to the world—but also its missed opportunity. For centuries, Chinese inventors and generals pushed the limits of explosive and naval technology. Yet internal politics, conservatism, and fear of militarization later dulled their edge. What began as **world-leading innovation** gradually became history's warning: **inventing the future doesn't matter if you don't keep building it**.

Chapter 14: The Philosophy of War in China

14.1 The Art of War and Its Legacy

How Sun Tzu's Ideas Shaped Battles, Empires, and the Modern World

In the realm of military thought, few texts rival the influence of **Sun Tzu's** *The Art of War*. Written during the turbulent Warring States period, this slim volume became the **strategic bible** not only for Chinese generals, but eventually for politicians, business leaders, and military theorists across the world. At its core, *The Art of War* isn't about brute strength—it's about **mastering the mind, the moment, and the enemy.**

Key Principles of Strategy

Sun Tzu emphasized **deception, adaptability, and psychological control** over force. His lessons were about war, but also about **how to win without fighting**—the highest form of victory.

- **Deception** is central. "All warfare is based on deception," Sun Tzu wrote. Misdirection, false retreats, and feigned weaknesses allowed smaller forces to defeat stronger enemies.

- **Adaptability** was crucial. A commander must move like water—shaping strategy to terrain, weather, morale, and timing. Rigid plans collapse; flexible minds survive.

- The famous maxim, **"Know your enemy and know yourself, and you need not fear the result of a hundred battles,"** emphasized intelligence, introspection, and preparation. Strategy begins **before the first arrow flies.**

Importantly, Sun Tzu highlighted **morale and leadership** as decisive factors. Armies don't break from weapons—they break from within.

Historical Applications

Across dynasties, Chinese generals put Sun Tzu's principles into practice—sometimes subtly, sometimes with theatrical brilliance.

- At the **Battle of Red Cliffs**, the allied forces of Sun Quan and Liu Bei outwitted Cao Cao's numerically superior army with fire attacks, psychological tricks, and control of the river. They didn't overpower Cao Cao—they **unraveled his confidence**.

- **Zhuge Liang**, the iconic strategist of the Three Kingdoms period, embodied Sun Tzu's wisdom. His famed **"Empty Fort Strategy,"** in which he tricked a larger force into retreating by calmly playing music in an undefended city, remains a textbook example of psychological warfare.

- During the **Ming dynasty**, defensive strategy against the Mongols relied not on constant combat, but on **managing resources, anticipating attacks, and building fortifications** that neutralized cavalry advantages. It was slow, deliberate war—not for glory, but for survival.

These strategies were often misunderstood as passive or evasive. In truth, they reflected a deeper philosophy: **control the conditions, and the battle will fight itself**.

Global Influence

The Art of War did not remain confined to China. Over centuries, it traveled across cultures and disciplines.

- In the 20th and 21st centuries, it became essential reading in **Western military academies**, boardrooms, and political science programs. Generals, CEOs, and even politicians regularly cite Sun Tzu when describing campaign strategy or business maneuvering.

- In **modern warfare**, Sun Tzu's ideas about intelligence, disruption, and psychological dominance echo in everything from **cyberwarfare to drone campaigns**. Victory now often comes from **disabling infrastructure or morale**, not occupation.

- The book has been applied in **competitive sports, negotiations, corporate strategy**, and even personal development. Its power lies in **timeless insights on conflict and control**, relevant anywhere people clash.

Sun Tzu didn't write about gunpowder, tanks, or satellites—but his work still shapes them. *The Art of War* endures because it isn't just a manual for war—it's a **manual for winning in life's most difficult arenas**. And in China's military tradition, it remains the soul of strategy—a reminder that strength without clarity is often the greatest weakness.

14.2 Legalism and Confucian Tensions

Order, Morality, and the Ethics of Command

While *The Art of War* laid the groundwork for strategic thinking, ancient China's military doctrines were also shaped by deeper philosophical tensions—especially between **Legalism and Confucianism**, with Daoist thought offering a quieter but powerful alternative. These systems didn't just define how wars were fought—they influenced **who fought them, why, and under what limits**.

Legalist Control and Command

Legalism, dominant during the Qin dynasty and influential in other authoritarian regimes, saw war as an extension of **absolute state control**.

- It emphasized **strict discipline**. Under Legalist rule, armies operated like machines—every unit controlled, every failure punished. Disobedience on the battlefield could result in execution, not just of the offender but of their entire unit.

- **Punishment-based leadership** was seen as the most reliable way to ensure order. Incentives existed—especially for killing enemy soldiers—but **fear of reprisal** was the primary motivator.

- This translated into a **rigid military hierarchy**, where command flowed from the top with no room for interpretation. Generals followed orders without deviation, even if conditions changed.

Legalist militaries could be brutally efficient, but often lacked **initiative and moral flexibility**, especially in prolonged conflicts or unconventional warfare.

Confucian Restraint and Moral Limits

Confucianism, more influential during the Han and later dynasties, took a starkly different approach. It valued **ethical governance, civilian supremacy**, and **moral clarity**—even in war.

- War was never glorified. It was seen as a necessary evil that should only be pursued when **all peaceful options had failed**. Victory was not just about defeating enemies, but about maintaining social harmony.

- Confucian doctrine taught that **civilian officials should restrain military power**, and that soldiers, while necessary, ranked below scholars and administrators in social importance.

- Leaders were expected to weigh **moral consequences**, not just strategic outcomes. Massacres, deception, and cruelty were frowned upon unless absolutely unavoidable.

This created a paradox: Confucian states were **slow to mobilize**, but when they did, they often fought with **a strong sense of national or ethical justification**—which could increase troop morale and civilian support.

Daoist Flexibility and Harmony

Although less dominant politically, Daoist thinking quietly informed Chinese battlefield decisions—especially in elite or unconventional units.

- Daoism encouraged commanders to **avoid unnecessary conflict**. Victory was best achieved through manipulation of terrain, timing, and energy—not direct confrontation.

- The Daoist ideal was to "win without fighting." When battle was unavoidable, Daoism taught to **flow around the enemy** like water around stone, exploiting weaknesses with minimal force.

- Nature was not something to conquer—it was **an ally**. Daoist generals paid close attention to **weather, geography, and seasonal cycles**, using fog, rivers, and winds as part of their toolkit.

In many cases, Daoism influenced **ambush tactics, guerrilla movements**, and long-term siege strategies—emphasizing patience, subtlety, and avoidance of prolonged bloodshed.

Together, these three philosophies created a **deeply complex military culture**. Legalism drilled discipline, Confucianism restrained cruelty, and Daoism urged strategic creativity. No single view dominated forever—but Chinese warfare was always more than swords and arrows. It was **a question of ethics, balance, and control**, where victory wasn't just about surviving the battle—but doing so with honor, harmony, and the empire's soul intact.

14.3 Strategic Thinking Across Eras

Commanders as Philosophers, Victory as Harmony

In the West, generals are often remembered for tactics and triumphs. In China, many were remembered for something deeper: **their philosophy**. Across dynasties, strategic thinking was seen not merely as military logic—but as **moral and cosmic alignment**, where the right decision could restore order, and the wrong one could bring ruin to an entire dynasty.

Chinese generals weren't just warriors. They were **statesmen, scholars, and philosophers**, expected to weigh every move against history, ethics, and the will of heaven.

The General as Philosopher

Great commanders like **Wu Qi, Sun Bin, and Zhuge Liang** weren't celebrated just for winning battles—they were revered for **writing doctrine, enforcing ethics, and embodying discipline**.

- **Wu Qi** trained troops with brutal equality—forcing generals to sleep on the ground and eat soldier rations. His reforms emphasized merit and accountability.

- **Sun Bin**, a descendant of Sun Tzu's school, used deception, calculation, and clever positioning—not brute force—to defeat superior armies, most famously at the Battle of Maling.

- **Zhuge Liang** blended Confucian morality with strategic brilliance. His campaigns were cautious but elegant—always seeking balance between ambition and caution.

For these men, **command decisions were moral acts**. Every movement on the battlefield was a reflection of judgment, restraint, and a sense of greater duty. **A battle won dishonorably was a defeat in spirit.**

Balance of Offense and Defense

One of the central tenets of Chinese strategic thought is knowing when **not** to fight.

- Commanders learned to ask: **When to strike?** When is the enemy weak, the weather right, the terrain favorable?

- **When to retreat?** Not as defeat, but as repositioning. Sun Tzu wrote, "A skilled commander wins first, then goes to war." Sometimes, the best fight was the one postponed.

- **When to wait?** Patience was a weapon. Entire campaigns were decided by who could hold back longer, letting impatience weaken their opponent.

This balance wasn't just tactical—it was **existential**. It reflected harmony between man and moment. Aggression without timing was considered reckless. Restraint without intent was weakness.

The Role of Fate and Cosmic Signs

Beyond battlefield logic, strategy in ancient China was shaped by belief in **fate, omens, and celestial approval.**

- **Astrology and omens** often guided the timing of campaigns. Eclipses, animal behavior, or dreams could delay invasions or signal divine disapproval.

- Generals sought **ancestral approval** before major campaigns. Temples were consulted, rituals performed, and sacrifices made to ensure moral clarity.

- The **Mandate of Heaven**, the core justification for rule in imperial China, extended to warfare. Victory was proof of divine favor; defeat was a sign the regime had lost legitimacy.

This didn't mean Chinese warfare lacked logic or discipline—but it operated within a **moral-spiritual framework** that gave war both higher meaning and stricter boundaries.

In ancient China, strategy was never just about weapons, formations, or numbers. It was about **judgment, virtue, and harmony**. A general had to think like a philosopher, act like a sage, and strike like thunder—only when the moment was right. For in Chinese thought, the true purpose of war was not conquest, but **restoration of balance**—and the greatest victories left the sword unsheathed.

Chapter 15: Lessons for the Modern World

15.1 Timeless Military Principles

What Ancient China Teaches Modern Commanders, CEOs, and Strategists

Over 3,000 years of Chinese military history produced far more than battles and borders—it produced principles. These ideas helped build empires and also explained why they collapsed. Surprisingly, they remain just as powerful in today's age of data, drones, and diplomacy. From ancient palaces to modern boardrooms, the **timeless lessons of Chinese warfare** are not about destruction—but survival, adaptability, and psychological superiority.

Adapt or Die

If there's one universal rule from Chinese military history, it's this: **adapt or perish**.

- Successful dynasties like the Han, Tang, and early Ming **embraced reform**. They improved weapons, rotated generals, and shifted tactics based on their enemies—whether Mongol cavalry or nomadic raiders.

- In contrast, regimes that resisted change—like late Qing China—**collapsed under pressure**, clinging to outdated tactics, ignoring foreign advances, and fearing internal innovation.

- Adaptation wasn't just technological. It was structural. The best generals weren't the most brutal—they were the most **flexible**, both on the battlefield and in command.

Reform isn't optional. It's the difference between **lasting a dynasty or losing one**.

The Price of Stagnation

History's harshest punishment is reserved for those who stop evolving.

- The Song Dynasty had advanced gunpowder weapons but failed to mass-produce or innovate further. Their reluctance to empower generals or decentralize command led to **slow, bureaucratic defeats**.

- The Qing refused to modernize despite growing Western threats. Their neglect of the navy and dismissal of foreign arms cost them in the **Opium Wars and Boxer Rebellion**.

- Every downfall shared the same pattern: **a failure to listen, adjust, and lead through change**.

In today's world, where industries can collapse overnight, the same principle applies. **Inaction kills more than failure.**

Learning from Failure

Chinese commanders were expected not only to fight—but to **reflect**. Losses weren't just setbacks. They were **data**.

- After the defeat at the **Battle of Fei River**, Eastern Jin generals reevaluated their defensive strategies, helping them hold the south for decades longer.

- The Ming Dynasty's loss in the **Tumu Crisis** exposed poor logistics and overconfidence—leading to later investment in forts and communication chains.

- **Every failure triggered reform**—or hastened collapse, depending on whether lessons were absorbed.

The best strategists didn't fear failure. They **interrogated it**.

Intelligence Wins Battles

From the Warring States to the Han, one truth was constant: **the side with better information won.**

- Ancient China made use of **spies, defectors, intercepted letters**, and disinformation long before modern espionage existed.

- Sun Tzu emphasized this: "If you know the enemy and know yourself, you need not fear the result of a hundred battles."

- Timing was everything—armies that moved one day earlier often rewrote history. Those who acted blindly? Forgotten.

War isn't about force. It's about **precision**.

Psychological Edge and Non-Violent Victories

The most celebrated generals in Chinese history didn't just kill—they manipulated.

- **Zhuge Liang's Empty Fort Strategy**, where he tricked a larger force into retreating by acting unafraid, is still taught in military schools worldwide.

- Many victories came from **alliances, misdirection, terrain control**, and even silence. Avoiding battle was often seen as a **superior outcome**.

- The goal of warfare wasn't destruction—it was **restoration of order with minimal loss**.

Ancient Chinese warfare wasn't about conquest. It was about **longevity**—of dynasties, of systems, of civilization itself. And in a modern world filled with complexity, competition, and uncertainty, these principles offer a stark reminder: **the greatest victories are earned not with strength—but with insight.**

15.2 Cultural Memory of Warfare

How Ancient Battles Still Shape Modern Minds

In China, war is not just history—it's **cultural DNA**. Battles fought thousands of years ago still echo through classrooms, novels, and national consciousness. Military defeat and victory alike have been transformed into **stories, symbols, and strategies,** carried forward not only by scholars but by the people. This collective memory doesn't just preserve the past—it subtly **guides modern values, leadership, and even foreign policy.**

National Pride and Trauma

War left scars—but also pride.

- The **Great Wall**, built to keep out northern invaders, remains more than just stone—it is a **monument to endurance**, discipline, and unity in the face of centuries of nomadic threats.

- Cultural heroes like **Yue Fei**, a Song general known for his loyalty and resistance to the Jurchen Jin, symbolize **unbreakable patriotism**. His tattooed back—"Serve the country with utmost loyalty"—is etched into national folklore.

- But not all memories are proud. The **losses to Western powers during the Opium Wars**, and the humiliation under colonial pressures, continue to fuel modern narratives of **"never again."**

This dual legacy—**glory and grief**—continues to shape national resilience and suspicion toward foreign influence.

Literature and Storytelling

No other country has turned its wars into literature with such lasting cultural power.

- **Romance of the Three Kingdoms**, one of the Four Great Classical Novels, blends history and myth from the chaotic collapse of the Han Dynasty. It's not just read—it's quoted in business meetings, referenced in films, and taught in schools.

- This story, filled with brilliant strategists, flawed heroes, and tragic defeats, gave China enduring archetypes: **the cunning tactician, the loyal warrior, the tragic ruler.**

- Lessons from war are embedded in legend: **Deception over brute force, loyalty over ambition, timing over speed.**

This makes military history **accessible to every generation**, not just through facts—but through **emotion and narrative.**

Education and Modern Use

Warfare isn't just remembered—it's **institutionalized** in education and leadership.

- Chinese **military academies** still teach *The Art of War* and the campaigns of Zhuge Liang and Wei Qing—not just for inspiration, but as **practical decision-making frameworks**.

- Business schools and management training programs incorporate **military analogies**, teaching executives how to "divide and conquer" markets or "strike the enemy where they are weakest."

- Even foreign policy reflects this mindset: **long-term patience, indirect influence, and strategic silence** are valued traits rooted in ancient command philosophy.

Unlike many modern nations, China sees strategy not as a specialty—but as a **national skill**, honed by centuries of war, legend, and reflection.

Ancient Chinese warfare wasn't forgotten—it was **woven into the national story**. From stone walls to boardroom strategy, from battlefield legends to high school history classes, the memory of war continues to guide thought and identity.

In the end, China's greatest weapon may not have been its armies—but its **ability to remember**. To learn. To turn trauma into teaching, and victory into vision.

15.3 The Enduring Legacy

How Ancient Chinese Warfare Still Shapes East Asia and Global Strategy

Long after the last imperial army marched, the influence of Chinese warfare endures—**not just in China, but across East Asia**, and increasingly in global military thinking. From Japan's samurai code to modern policy in Beijing, the echoes of Sun Tzu, Legalist military codes, and dynastic campaigns continue to ripple through **strategy, diplomacy, and doctrine.**

Influence on East Asian Warfare

China's strategic legacy helped define the **military cultures of Japan, Korea, and Vietnam**.

- In Japan, early samurai doctrine borrowed heavily from Chinese concepts of **moral war, hierarchy, and ritualized combat**, especially during the Asuka and Nara periods. *The Art of War* was studied by daimyo (warlords) throughout the Sengoku era.

- Korea adopted Chinese-style military bureaucracy during the Goryeo and Joseon periods, blending Confucian values with a centralized command model.

- Vietnam, while often resisting Chinese domination, absorbed Chinese siege tactics, bureaucracy, and even language into its war doctrine. Ironically, China's long attempts at conquest made

Vietnam **one of the most tactically flexible and hardened military cultures in the region.**

This regional exchange wasn't one-sided—it was a **dialogue of influence**, shaped by geography, war, and centuries of diplomacy.

Modern Parallels

China's ancient strategic logic remains remarkably relevant in today's **age of information, hybrid warfare, and asymmetric conflict.**

- **Information warfare**—a modern battlefield that relies on deception, manipulation, and timing—echoes Sun Tzu's emphasis on **misdirection, psychological dominance, and preemptive action.**

- In **asymmetric warfare**, where weaker forces use intelligence, mobility, or terrain to neutralize stronger ones, we see the enduring relevance of tactics used by rebels, river-based armies, and frontier defenders throughout Chinese history.

- Leadership under pressure, a recurring theme from **Zhuge Liang to Yue Fei**, continues to guide discussions on **crisis management, loyalty, and resilience** in both military and civilian command roles.

The tools have changed. The principles haven't.

China's Military Future

Modern China draws heavily on its **strategic memory** when making geopolitical decisions. The past is not forgotten—it's **weaponized**.

- The **Belt and Road Initiative**, framed as economic infrastructure, also mirrors ancient **military logic**: secure trade routes, fortify chokepoints, and build long-term leverage over rivals. It's **Silk Road 2.0**, with defensive logic baked into economic expansion.

- China's modern military reforms—streamlining command, investing in tech, emphasizing mobility—mirror past dynasties that rose through **reform and failed through rigidity**.

- The continued use of **The Art of War** in military academies, political rhetoric, and even artificial intelligence research shows that **strategy remains cultural**, not just institutional.

China does not see strategy as episodic. It sees it as **civilizational**.

In the end, the legacy of ancient Chinese warfare is not about glorifying war. It's about **understanding power**—how it's earned, preserved, and lost. From bamboo scrolls to cyber warfare, from walled cities to maritime disputes, the same rules apply:

Know yourself. Know your enemy. Win without fighting if you can. And never forget the lessons of history—because your rivals won't.

Printed in Dunstable, United Kingdom